PARLIAMENTS AND ESTATES IN EUROPE TO 1789

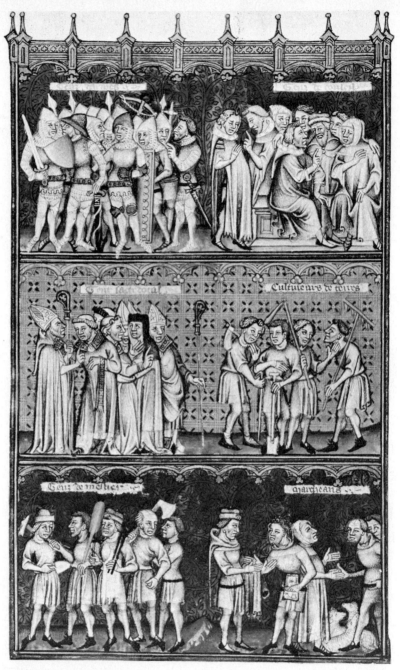

1 A society organized into 'orders', corporations and gilds is symbolized in a four-teenth-century MS. depicting (reading downwards) soldiers, councillors, clerics, peasants, craftsmen and merchants.

PARLIAMENTS AND ESTATES IN EUROPE
TO 1789

A. R. MYERS

with 79 illustrations

HARCOURT BRACE JOVANOVICH, INC.

For Ruth

Picture research by Alla Weaver

© 1975 THAMES AND HUDSON LTD, LONDON

First American edition 1975

ISBN 0–15–568123–0

Library of Congress Catalog Card Number: 75–789

Printed and bound in Great Britain by Jarrold and Sons Ltd, Norwich

CONTENTS

PREFACE

I should like first of all to thank Professor Geoffrey Barraclough for inviting me to write this volume and for valuable editorial comments when the manuscript was presented. I am grateful to Professor John Roskell for reading the manuscript of this book and for the useful suggestions which he then made. I have benefited from the help of Mr Roderick Tann, who assisted me in compiling the index. I owe much to the skilful labours of various members of the editorial staff of Thames and Hudson, in preparing the manuscript for the press, in finding appropriate pictures, in designing the volume, and in seeing the book into print. If the practice of the firm had permitted, I would have mentioned them by name; as it is, I thank them in general, but very cordial, terms.

I should also like to acknowledge with gratitude the help of the British Academy towards the expenses of writing this book.

A. R. MYERS

University of Liverpool
April 1975

2 Charles VII of France at a *Lit de Justice*, 1458. This was a session of the *parlement* – the highest judicial court in the land – presided over by the monarch.

I OBLIGATION AND PRIVILEGE: THE AGE OF ESTATES

The rapidly changing world of the twentieth century has forced historians to reconsider their view of European history. The old landmarks of 1485 in English history, and of 1494 in European, are now seen to have lost their significance sixty years ago, with the outbreak of the First World War. In their stead historians have suggested different periodizations, put forward from varying points of view. But in English-speaking countries historians have not in general realized, to the same extent as their colleagues on the continent of Europe have done, the importance of 'estates' in the history of Latin Christendom. This may be because in Britain the estates never developed so fully, with such distinctive legal rights, as they did in most European countries. Yet on the continent of Europe, west of Russia and the Balkans, the five centuries before 1789 might well be called 'the Age of the Estates', the great link between the age of feudalism and the modern world.

The age of the estates was a period in which the normal form of government was a monarchy ruling over a society dominated by 'orders', 'corps' or bodies, corporations, colleges, and societies, each with important duties and privileges. As the *avocat du roi*, Séguier, expressed it in the *lit de justice** held on 12 March 1776 by Louis XVI at the *Parlement de Paris*: 'The clergy, the nobility, the highest courts, the lower tribunals, the officers attached to these tribunals, the universities, the academies, the financial and commercial companies, all present, in all parts of the state, living bodies which one can consider as links in a great chain of which the first link is in the hands of Your Majesty, as head and highest administrator of all that makes up the body of the nation.' It was part of a moving defence of the *ancien régime*, ardently supported by the *Parlement*, against the king's intention, on the advice of his minister, Turgot, to suppress the gilds of arts and crafts, in the interests of free trade. However much such a move might be applauded by *philosophes* and radical reformers, Séguier and the *parlementaires* saw the move as the beginning of the

9

---

* The most solemn session of the *Parlement*, when the king presided in person and could override any decision of the *Parlement*.

3 *(Left)* Emblem of the gild of tailors of Stuttgart, 1713.

4 *(Opposite)* Henry VIII presenting a charter to the barber-surgeons. To secure rights and privileges from the Crown was one of the gild's functions.

end of their world. They were right; between 1789 and 1791 all privileged corporations, of whatever kind, were abolished. Henceforth France, one and indivisible, would recognize only the rights of individual citizens, all free and equal in the eyes of the law; and the French Revolution was to carry this dynamite throughout Europe.

The old society which was to be either blown up or stiffened into resistance by such a concept thought of itself as a living tissue of legal bodies based on a social concept of authority and on a deliberately unequal, hierarchical ideal of society; all of them enjoyed liberties based partly on custom and partly on contractual rights, recognized in formal law. Lesser and more sharply defined bodies were thought of as groups in greater and looser bodies, known as 'orders' or 'estates'. In the developed form of such a society the estates that were officially recognized usually numbered three, and occasionally four. There were the clergy, usually regarded as the first estate; for though in its last generations the *ancien régime* in France contained an anti-clerical and sceptical element, though Louis XVI had to object to the nomination of the Archbishop of Toulouse, Loménie de Brienne, as Archbishop of Paris on the ground that he preferred a prelate who

believed in God, the old society never formally abandoned its respect for the primacy of the spiritual sphere, as represented by the Church. Then there was the nobility, sometimes divided formally into higher and lesser nobility; and however tamed the nobility might become politically, socially it maintained its privileges and dominance unimpaired until the end of the old régime. There was the bourgeoisie, organized in chartered towns, in companies of merchants, in gilds of craftsmen, in academies of savants, in chambers of advocates, attorneys, notaries, and magistrates, in societies of doctors, surgeons, apothecaries, all entrenched in privileges. Occasionally there were, as in Sweden or Friesland, officially recognized estates of peasants, though it was usually only influential and prosperous peasants who were deemed worthy of rights and privileges in a formal estate.

So characteristic were these estates and corporations of west European culture between the thirteenth and the eighteenth century that German historians have dubbed this form of state and society the *Ständestaat*. This is so neat and clear compared with the cumbrous and ambiguous English equivalent, 'the state or society of the

5 The foundation of New College, Oxford, by William of Wykeham in 1380.

6 Eighteenth-century town assembly in Appenzell, Switzerland. This kind of grass-roots democracy was not as effective as impressionable foreigners – including Rousseau – believed.

corporations and estates', that henceforth it will be used in this book to describe this form of European culture. The *Ständestaat* is not only characteristic of this period of history, but is probably unique to western Europe. This is because the various ingredients which created it came together in the necessary way only in Latin Christendom.

In the Dark Ages the vacuum of authority, created by the collapse of the western Roman Empire and the weakness and instability of the barbarian kingdoms, was filled to some extent by the Catholic Church. This not only put it in a strong position to judge the moral authority of rulers, a role that it retained until nearly the end of the *ancien régime*; it was also able to give a powerful impetus to the tendency

in western Europe to stress the importance of law in public relations. The Catholic Church inherited in especially strong measure Roman notions of justice and legal definition. These ideas were not so fully developed in the Dark Ages as they were later to become; but they could already be seen at work, moulding barbarian notions of kingship to a new model of the just ruler, and shaping the relationships of kindred with kindred and lords with dependents. Already they helped to give a more ordered and contractual aspect to the relationship of abbot and monk, and to the relationship of the monastery to the Church, in monastic communities of the Roman obedience, than was the case in either Celtic or Byzantine monasticism. The role which the Benedictine monasteries won for themselves in Latin Christendom, combining subordination of the individual to the group with the privileges of the group in relation to the outer world,

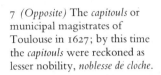
was to be of importance in developing the idea of legalized associations
within the Church, and hence eventually of the concept of the
Ständestaat.

Then in the ninth and tenth centuries came the development in the
Frankish empire of the institutions of feudalism. Amid all the
tumult and uncertainty of life, feudal institutions encouraged the
idea of an ordered, hierarchical society. Suzerain and vassal each had
his duties and his privileges; they had a contractual relationship,
symbolized and solemnized in the ceremony of homage, fealty, and
investiture. This ceremony could be, and was, compared to the
sacrament of marriage, which also involved the exchange of solemn
promises, and created very definite judicial obligations and legal
rights, to endure as long as life itself. The tenth and eleventh centuries
saw the spreading in the west of the network of feudal relations, and the

15

increasing depth and intricacy of their impact on society. Not only between prince and tenants-in-chief, but between principal and lesser tenants, they emphasized the idea of specified dependent tenure in return for definite services. They enabled lords who had skill, cunning and luck on their side to develop territorial states. These necessitated more officials, with growing powers, to keep the state together, to enforce the will of the ruler, and to increase his authority. They were aided by the great influx of Greek, Roman and Arabic learning in the eleventh and twelfth centuries. This knowledge not only enhanced the technical means of government, as in financial and secretarial expertise, and increased considerably the number of educated persons capable of forming a devoted bureaucracy; there was also a remarkable revival in the knowledge of Roman law and in more exalted concepts of royal authority in administration and in law-making. Royal officials began to quote more frequently tags of Roman law, such as *Rex est imperator in regno suo* and *Quod principi placuit, legis habet vigorem.*★

But the increase in royal authority was only gradual and uneven, and many of the techniques and concepts that it could use were available, at this stage, to other forces in contemporary society. Churchmen could employ the new learning, with its improved methods of logic, its sharpened awareness of the Church's traditions, real or fictitious, its stress on law, its emphasis on the responsibility of the law given to God and the Church, to bring kings under judgment. New monastic orders accepted the Benedictine concept of strict obligations within and privileges without, based on law and contract. Not only were they prepared, with papal backing, to defy princes who seemed to them to ignore the teachings of Christ and to jeopardize the welfare of the Church; by their very existence and cohesion they encouraged the notion that groups of men, within their proper sphere, might rightfully enjoy, as a group, privileges which ought to be respected by both Church and state. With the development simultaneously of canon law and of creative vitality in the Church, other groups acquired legal status: cathedral chapters, colleges, universities, and religious gilds. Bishops and abbots became more aware of their duties and rights, not simply as individuals, but as members of an order. This awareness emboldened them to take a more concerted and independent attitude towards the prince. Even in a state where the king was strong, as in the England of Henry II, one can see how,

★ 'The king is an emperor in his own realm' and 'What pleases the prince has the force of law.'

9 St Benedict. The monastic order he founded combined the subordination of the individual with the privileged position of the group.

during the Becket controversy, bishops and abbots had become conscious of the privileges of their order, feared though the king might be. In a state where the king was weak, as in twelfth- and thirteenth-century Denmark, the bishops could defy and judge kings with impunity. And if royal officials could remember the tag *Quod principi placuit, legis habet vigorem*, churchmen could recall that *Quod omnes tangit, ab omnibus approbetur.*★

Nobles, too, faced with the increasing power and demands of the prince, were prompted to take concerted action to win and to defend common privileges, conscious as they were of feudal notions as to the duties of the overlord and of the Church's teaching on the obligations of the ruler within a framework of law and custom. They insisted on their right to be tried by their peers, to enjoy hunting rights, to be protected from disparagement, degrading punishments or work, and direct taxation, and to be consulted on proposed changes of custom. If the ruler appeared to be ignoring local customs and institutions in

18

★ 'That which touches everyone, let everyone approve.'

10 (*Opposite*) King Henry VI, appointing John Talbot, Earl of Shrewsbury, Constable of France, presents him with the sword of office. Investiture symbolized and made manifest the relationship between overlord and vassal.

11 (*Right*) The martyrdom of Becket. The 'turbulent priest' typified the Church's God-given right to judge the king.

order to build up a centralized monarchy, they might band together to demand a confirmation of the privileges of the region and especially of its nobility. So persuasive was this point of view, so dominant became the notion in Latin Christendom of the subjection of the ruler to law and custom, that such common action of nobles was practised even in countries, such as Hungary, which had not experienced feudal relationships. Whether by concerted rebellion, collective petition, or both, the nobles of various countries and regions succeeded in extorting charters from rulers, from the charter of Ottokar to the nobles of Styria in 1186, or the Golden Bull granted by Andrew II of Hungary in 1222, to the Pact of Koszyce for the Polish nobility conceded by King Ludwig in 1374, and the diploma for the nobility of the empire delivered by the Emperor Sigismund in 1422.

Churchmen and nobles were not the only groups in society to develop a sense of common interests and a demand for the recognition of corporate privileges. The centuries that saw the growth of canon law

12 *(Above)* The Comte de Foix giving orders to his huntsmen, from a fifteenth-century miniature. Hunting rights were among the privileges the nobility jealously guarded against royal encroachment.

13 *(Opposite)* Sigismund, Holy Roman Emperor, from whom the nobles of the empire received their diploma of rights and privileges in 1422.

and the recovery of Roman law saw also the revival of trade. Towns swelled in size in the twelfth and thirteenth centuries all over western Europe. Their leading members were in especially urgent need of recognition of a common identity and corporate privileges. Townsmen were gaining wealth in a society dominated by aristocratic, clerical, and rural values and modes of life. Burgesses needed official recognition of special forms of urban land tenure, free from servile or rural obligations, and of special town customs and courts, adapted to the demands of trade. They wanted protection from exploitation by royal or seigniorial officials. Merchants venturing away from their native towns on trading missions desired to have mutual support, legally recognized and enforced, not only from casual robbers or pirates, but from the predatory instincts of barons or princes through whose territories they had to pass. So, by combining together, townsmen set to work to acquire corporate privileges for their town and their order. If the monarchy was strong, as in England, the leading towns might look to the king for charters of liberties for individual towns (or for confirmation of charters granted by lesser lords), though even here societies of merchants eventually won corporate privileges, as with the Merchants of the Staple or the Merchant Adventurers. If the monarchy was weak, as in thirteenth- and fourteenth-century Scotland and Germany, then towns might have to join together in leagues and sometimes wage war to gain or to defend the privileges they valued.

It was necessary for these orders – clergy, nobles, and townsmen – to come to terms with the ruler. Where the Crown was, on the whole, increasing in power, as in twelfth- and thirteenth-century England and France, it might be necessary for the estates to insist on definition as a safeguard against erosion of liberties, whether written or customary. Where the Crown was weak in authority, as in thirteenth- and fourteenth-century Poland and Scandinavia, the estates could afford to take a more independent and aggressive line. But if the orders had to come to terms with the ruler, the ruler had to come to terms with the estates, for they wielded much economic and social power and the climate of opinion favoured their claims. If the monarchy eventually gained in power, after many set-backs, as in France, Spain or Austria, the Crown harnessed the estates to its service, but at the price of confirming and respecting many of their privileges, such as the exemption of nobles from taxation, the special position of churchmen in society, and the important rights of urban oligarchs over the trade of their town or region. If, on the other hand, the monarchy found itself in constant difficulties, as in Scotland down to 1603 or in Denmark until 1660, or lost ground, as in Poland and in Hungary in the fifteenth and sixteenth centuries, the estates advanced their claims – particularly the estate in the most favourable position to gain power, that of the nobility.

In view of the growing power and cohesion of the estates in the thirteenth and fourteenth centuries, it became politic for princes to consult leading members of each order in assemblies where questions of war, justice, administration, and taxation might be raised. Such assemblies might be organized for the whole of a prince's territories or for significant regions of them. The leading members might appear in the assemblies either by virtue of their office or status, or because of election; and the groups they represented were at first the dominant estates in contemporary society, the clergy and nobles, soon to be joined by the towns. At first the composition and functions of such assemblies were very ill defined and fluid, but gradually they solidified into increasingly definite forms which, in a traditionally-minded society, came to be regarded as customary and therefore to be respected. On the continent of Europe the members of the assemblies usually represented orders and grouped themselves in separate 'houses' accordingly. Sometimes these were called 'estates', from the orders they represented (*état, stato, éstament, staat, staet*); sometimes they were named 'members' of estates (*brazo, braccio, lid*). In any case the connection with the orders of society was close and obvious.

THE MEANING OF REPRESENTATION

The historians who have worked with the International Commission for the History of Representative and Parliamentary Institutions have done much in the last forty years to show the importance and ubiquity of these assemblies in Latin Christendom from the thirteenth century onwards. Nevertheless, in the English-speaking world the importance of these institutions is still insufficiently appreciated. There is probably some awareness of the political role enjoyed, at varying periods between the thirteenth and the eighteenth century, by the *Cortes* of Aragon, the States-General of the Netherlands, the *Riksdag* of Sweden; but too often the Estates-General of France is still regarded as typical, whereas its history was in many ways exceptional. Among the misconceptions about the old parliaments of Europe are the notions that representative assemblies on the continent of Europe before the French Revolution were rare, transient, narrow in basis, and weak in power. All these suppositions are untrue.

Far from representative institutions being rare in Europe before 1789, they flourished at one time or another in every realm of Latin Christendom. They first emerge clearly towards the end of the twelfth century in the Spanish kingdom of Leon, in the thirteenth century in Castile, Aragon (and also Catalonia and Valencia), Portugal, Sicily, the Empire and some of its constituent states such as Brandenburg and Austria, and in England and Ireland. In the fourteenth century parliaments developed in France (in many of the provinces and for a large part of the realm), the Netherlands, Scotland, more of the German and Italian states, and Hungary; in the fifteenth century representative Estates appeared in Denmark, Sweden, and Poland.

As to the duration of these institutions, the preceding survey will have indicated that in most of Latin Christendom parliaments appeared in the thirteenth or fourteenth centuries. Nearly all of them survived until the seventeenth or the early eighteenth century, and many were still meeting frequently when they were overwhelmed by the French Revolution. Some of them lasted in their old form into the nineteenth century; the Hungarian Diet was not reformed until 1848 and the Swedish *Riksdag* kept its four estates until 1866. In the Duchy of Mecklenburg the Estates continued to function, with frequent meetings and important powers, until 1918.

Another widespread misconception in Britain is that these older parliaments of Europe were very narrow in basis, assemblies which were concerned to defend the exclusive privileges of the minority groups that they represented; this explains, it is thought, why they foundered in contrast to the English Parliament and why they are worthy of less consideration. But two points need to be considered here. One is that before the Victorian Age the British Parliament itself rested, by twentieth-century standards, on a narrow basis, and if it represented 'the people' it did not claim to do so by virtue of election by the adult population. When, in the Army Council in 1647, Colonel Rainborough put forward the then extremist idea of universal suffrage, Cromwell voiced the general reaction, parliamentarian as well as royalist, in his indignant retort: 'Where is there any bound or

14 Fairfax presiding over the Army Council in 1647. It was in this body that Colonel Rainborough made the unwelcome suggestion of 'one man one vote'.

limit set if you take away this limit, that men have no interest but the interest of breathing shall have no voice in elections?'

The other consideration is that in their period of greatest virility – roughly the fourteenth and fifteenth centuries – these older European parliaments were commonly conceived to represent in a sense the whole population of the state, and they normally embraced all the elements that then mattered in politics. It was rare for peasants to be directly represented; and when they were, as in Sweden, Denmark, West Friesland, or the Tyrol, election was by a peasant élite. The deputies for the clergy were commonly conceived to speak for all the clergy, then a numerous group. The towns were sometimes thought of as representing not only the inhabitants of the town but those of the surrounding region as well. Sometimes some of the people of the neighbouring countryside actually participated in the election of the town deputies. Moreover, in the intensely aristocratic societies of the fourteenth and fifteenth centuries, juridical theory ordinarily conceived of the nobles as representing, in their capacity as territorial lords, the whole population of what was still a predominantly agrarian society (except in parts of the Low Countries and northern Italy), apart from those privileged orders who were represented separately, such as the clergy and chartered towns. However the parliament was organized, the nobles were nearly always an essential element in the days of its vigour, and usually a very powerful element. So, one way and another, these parliaments were commonly thought of as representing the whole realm. For example, at the *Cortes* of Lérida in 1301 Jaime II of Aragon held that the consent of the *Cortes* was the consent of the kingdom and that its decisions were therefore binding on all. Each session of the Castilian *Cortes* was called 'another kingdom' (*otro reino*). In Friuli (p. 93) the parliament was conceived to be representative of all the inhabitants of Friuli. In 1484 the chancellor of France described the Estates-General at Tours as representing the whole of the French people. Examples could be multiplied.

It is true that in many of the parliaments there was a tendency to shrinkage in the number either of estates or of persons within the estate. There was also a tendency to emphasize more strongly the privileges of the remaining groups. But the claim to represent a greater number of people in the realm was more widespread and persistent than is often realized. For example, by the sixteenth century the composition of the Castilian *Cortes* had dwindled to the repre-

26

15 Jaime II of Aragon and the *Cortes* of Barcelona.

big ... poctu marti noc
publica in barchinona et in tota alia
terra. et comin̄ oc̄ pre̅diceti domini
regis Aragonum. Qui hoc scribi fe̅c
et clausit die et anno q̅o supra. ◦

hic inapiunt constituciones statuta i
ordinaciones pace facie̅ge

16 Rembrandt's *Syndics of the Cloth Hall*, typical of the wealthy oligarchs who dominated the large towns in seventeenth-century Holland.

sentatives of eighteen towns, but these towns often claimed to stand for the different regions of Castile and hence to represent the whole realm except for the nobility and the clergy. In the United Netherlands, after the revolt from Spain and until the French Revolution, the provincial Estates of Holland gave a vote each to eighteen towns and only one vote to the nobles; but the nobles claimed to represent not only themselves but the rural districts and the small towns with no franchise. Not only did they claim this, but they were often supported by lesser folk in the struggles of the House of Orange against the wealthy 'regent' oligarchies that dominated the large towns. In the province of Zeeland the Estates consisted of seven members, six towns, and 'the first noble'; but the first noble was William the Silent, and thereafter his heirs, who claimed, and were usually felt, to represent the common people against the merchant oligarchies. In 1627 the estate of peasants was dropped from the Danish *Rigsdag*, partly on the ground that the peasants were adequately represented by the nobles.

In Poland the claims of the nobility had gone much further. Already by the latter half of the fourteenth century the claim had been advanced that the *corpus regni*, the body of active citizens, was restricted to the *communitas nobilium*, the nobility; and during the second half of the fifteenth century and the first half of the sixteenth century the bourgeoisie disappeared from the Diet, which came to consist (except for the king) entirely of nobility, on either a personal or a representative basis. From a twentieth-century viewpoint the claim of the nobility to represent the people may seem absurd, and even monstrous, a means of disguising and perpetuating the exploitation of the masses; but in the seventeenth century, and for most of the eighteenth century, it appeared a very justifiable point of view. So even the assemblies which seem patently narrow in basis to our twentieth-century minds, bred in notions of mass democracy, were apt to wear a different look before the ideas of the French Revolution struck root.

PARLIAMENTS AND THEIR POWERS

It is not correct moreover to think of European representative institutions as mainly weak, infrequent, and ineffective. It has sometimes been argued that the unique success and continuity of the English Parliament can be explained by its power over the purse and by its participation in legislation and justice. These are certainly factors; but they cannot constitute the whole story, for the most constant and important activity of these older parliaments in Europe was the granting of taxes, and a frequent attribute was participation in legislation. Almost everywhere in Latin Christendom the principle was, at one time or another, accepted by the rulers that, apart from the normal revenues of the prince, no taxes could be imposed without the consent of the parliament. The German saying that *Landtage sind Geldtage* – representative assemblies are financial assemblies – was applicable to nearly all these older parliaments. On this rock of financial control not only the English Parliament but many continental ones built an imposing edifice of power. It is true that from the middle of the fifteenth century onwards the Estates-General of France lost this control, as the *Cortes* of Castile began to do from the time of Ferdinand and Isabella; but in Britain this timing has often been taken as more typical of continental practice than it was, because many British parliamentary historians have scarcely looked for comparisons beyond France and Castile. The fact is that the Estates-General of

France and the *Cortes* of Castile were in this respect exceptional. Parliamentary control over exceptional taxation was usually more firmly established, more frequently exercised, and longer-lasting. In Germany, for example, in the fifteenth century the Estates of Brandenburg, Bavaria and Württemberg not only claimed the right to control taxation but at times took over the management of the prince's estates; by using their power of the purse they often influenced the ruler's policies, especially restraining him from military adventures. In many states the control over taxation lasted until the latter part of the seventeenth century, and in some cases it persisted until the French Revolution. The control of the Estates of Languedoc and Brittany over the right to tax was still vigorous in 1789; and in some states, such as Mecklenburg, Württemberg and Poland, the powers of the Estates actually increased during the seventeenth and eighteenth centuries.

It has also been assumed by some English historians that the English made unique discoveries of valuable levers to power in the shape of grants of supply made dependent on redress of grievances and of demands prepared in the form of Bills ready to become statutes as soon as they gained the royal assent. But both these methods were practised at one time or another in many continental assemblies – in Aragon, Catalonia, Valencia, the German principalities, Sweden, Bohemia, Hungary and Poland. The ruler usually retained the prerogative of doing a certain amount of law-making without the sanction of parliament, and sometimes the representative assembly, such as the French Estates-General, never gained the right to participate in the making of laws; though even in such cases the petitions and grievances of the Estates often provided material for law-making. But, on the other hand, the idea became widespread in western Europe that parliamentary approval ought to be obtained for all the more important laws. In fourteenth- and fifteenth-century Aragon not only was the consent of the *Cortes* essential for the making of all laws, but each parliamentary session ended with a *solio* or formal meeting of the king and the four *brazos* or estates in which all the measures of the session were solemnly proclaimed. This prevented the king from ignoring those activities of the *Cortes* which he did not like. Moreover, a committee of the *Cortes*, the *Diputación del Reyno*, usually composed of two members of each of the four *brazos* (clergy, magnates, *caballeros* or lesser nobility, and towns), was chosen to

17 Henry of Valois, elected King of Poland in 1573.

bridge the gaps between sessions of the *Cortes*, to watch over the enforcement of the laws, and to report back to the *Cortes* any breach of them.

In the Hungarian Diet in the sixteenth and seventeenth centuries the estates compiled a list of their demands and grievances (*postulata et gravamina*) on the basis of lists brought by deputies to the Diet. These demands and grievances were discussed by both houses, which had to agree before the final list was presented to the king. Without the consent of the Diet no Bill could be made law; though the king could, in favourable circumstances, issue ordinances on his own authority. In Poland, however, the control of the Diet over legislation became complete. The influence not only of the magnates but of the lesser nobility increased during the fifteenth and sixteenth centuries; and from the time of the capitulations of Henry of Valois on his election as king in 1573 the monarch was only one element in the Diet, whose consent to legislation was, in principle, no more important than that of the Senate (filled with great magnates) and the Chamber of Deputies (representing the rest of the nobility). By the middle of the seventeenth century the Polish Diet or *Sejm* had adopted the notorious

31

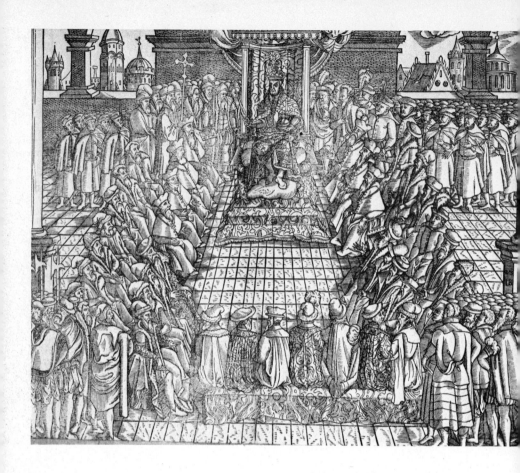

liberum veto, whereby a single member could, by his veto, not only prevent the passing of a law but secure the dissolution of the Diet. In this exaggerated form the anarchy of the Polish *Sejm* appears to have been unique; but the requirement of unanimity was not. We find a rule of unanimity for decisions in the *brazo* or estate of nobles in the *Cortes* of Valencia; on at least one occasion, in 1645, unanimity was reached there by throwing out a recalcitrant member into the street and then proceeding to a vote. In Aragon not only was the consent of the *Cortes* necessary to the making of all laws, but each of the four *brazos* had to come to a unanimous decision. This rule has caused some writers to exclaim that the enactment of any law in Aragon was nothing less than a miracle; but, more practical than the proud Polish nobility, the Aragonese *Cortes* often solved the problem by deciding

18 *(Opposite)* The Polish Diet, or *Sejm*, in 1590.

19 *(Right)* Queen Ulrika Eleonora, elected to the throne by the *Riksdag* after the death of her brother Charles XII.

much business by majority vote, or by referring the matter to a committee of four or more members from each *brazo*, with full power to act.

The Aragonese *Cortes* and the Polish *Sejm* not only resembled each other by having, at different periods, a great control over legislation and a unanimity rule for important decisions; they also possessed a function (shared by other assemblies) which, it is sometimes assumed, belonged to the English Parliament alone: they combined with the functions of a tax-granting and a legislative body those of a high court of justice, investigating wrongs done by the king or his officers to individuals or groups of individuals, of whatever rank, in defiance of the laws; and they had the right of demanding that justice should be done.

Finally, we should note that the functions of many parliaments were not limited to the granting of taxes, to legislation, and to justice. Varied powers were claimed by parliaments, especially in times of confusion and weakness in the government. Many parliaments, indeed most, asserted their views on the conduct of foreign relations at one time or another; they wanted to have a say in matters of war, peace, treaties and alliance. They often insisted on their right to appoint a regent for an infant prince, as happened in the treaty of 1489 between the Estates of Württemberg and Count Eberhard. They wanted to fix the succession to the throne if the royal line died out, or if there were a disputed succession, as happened in Sweden in 1719 with the election by the *Riksdag* of Ulrika Eleonora as queen. They tried to stipulate the terms on which each new ruler should be acknowledged on his accession, as occurred in Poland from 1573, or even, as in Pomerania and Aragon, to choose a new master if the ruler should break his promises or wrong his subjects. The history of most parliaments shows attempts to control the choice of the prince's advisers and ministers and to force on him a council nominated in parliament; in eighteenth-century Sweden *Sekreta Utskottet*, the 'Secret Committee' elected by the *Riksdag*, was for over a generation all-powerful, even against the king. Still more usual was the demand that parliaments should prescribe how the taxes should be spent, or should even undertake this collection and expenditure themselves through their own agents and treasury, as happened at various times with the *Országgyüles* or Diet of Hungary, the *Landtage* of some of the German principalities, or the Estates of Languedoc or Brittany. In some states, as, for example, Valencia and Jülich-Cleves, the assembly of estates at times claimed and exercised the right to meet for various purposes without a summons from the ruler.

REPRESENTATIVE ASSEMBLIES IN OTHER CULTURES
It should be clear from even this brief survey of the chief features of these older parliaments of Europe that the student of European civilization cannot afford to ignore them as unimportant. On the contrary, they are of great significance as expressions of important traits and forces in the development of the culture of western Europe. They are of all the greater interest in that they seem to be a characteristic of Latin Christendom; in their ubiquity and vigour they appear to be unique to the civilization of western Europe.

This is a point that has so far not attracted much attention in Britain; but it has aroused the interest of various German historians, especially Otto Hintze and Dietrich Gerhard. These historians have argued cogently that, before the spread of European influence over the rest of the world in the eighteenth and nineteenth centuries, the representative institutions of Latin Christendom were unique. The cities of ancient Greece and Rome were familiar with direct democracy but not with representative institutions, which indeed did not develop where the Roman tradition of the city state was strong, as in the republics of medieval Italy. There was no parallel in the absolute monarchies of the ancient civilizations of the Mediterranean or the Near East. An attempt has recently been made, by E. Szlechter, to see parallels in the empires of ancient Mesopotamia; but the activities of the assemblies of citizens and notables were usually judicial and administrative, at the behest of the king, and there is no evidence that either kind of assembly was elected. The Aryan invaders of India had a priesthood, a warrior aristocracy, and a peasantry, like the societies of early European civilization; but in the caste system which subsequently developed in India there was no soil to encourage the growth of representative institutions. The social rigidity of the caste system excluded a system of estates as in the west. Distinctions rested not on legally recognized privileges but on customary ranks, based on religious customs. In China the rise of privileged estates was prevented by the network of strong family ties, under patriarchal government. It is striking that in China there was no chivalric warrior aristocracy, which was so strong in the Estates of western Europe during their time of growth. It was impious to oppose the paternal and divine authority of the emperor, and the ruling bureaucracy of the mandarins was not a specially privileged class. Instead of representative opposition and control there was in China the occasional resistance of unorganized masses of people against oppression and misgovernment. Japanese and Muslim civilization passed through a phase not unlike that of European feudalism; but there was no corresponding flowering of assemblies of estates. Japanese feudalism was characterized by paternal authority, and strangers were incorporated into a Japanese war-band, not by the judicial concept of the feudal contract, but by being made honorary younger sons or brothers. The Shinto priests were too much bound up with the ancestor cult of the imperial house to form an estate and demand legal privileges. As for Islam, there was in its

35

feudalism no concept of judicial feudal contract but a religious duty to holy war; the spiritual leaders were part of the machinery of the state and could not lead an opposition to it.

Striking as is this difference between the institutions of Latin Christendom and those of other civilizations, it is even more remarkable that representative assemblies, as western Europe knew them, never developed in Byzantine or Russian civilization. It is remarkable because eastern European culture looked back to Graeco-Roman and Hebrew roots, as did that of the west; and if there is the theme of divergence from the west in Orthodox Europe there is also the theme of connection with it. It is true that in the Byzantine Empire popular assemblies were summoned from time to time by the government for fiscal matters. But those assemblies never had the right to legislate on fiscal or any other matters, and they were never allowed to criticize the government. It was only at times of revolution and revolutionary movements such as that of the Zealots (1341–50) that popular assemblies were able to oppose or even comment on the government; otherwise it was the Senate, the judges, the magistrates, and the emperor who formulated and applied state policy, and none of these had any representative character.

The Orthodox states of the Balkans need not detain us long. The first Bulgarian empire was too primitive in organization and outlook to develop a representative assembly; and after almost two centuries of Byzantine rule (1018–1186) the second Bulgarian state of the thirteenth and fourteenth centuries (1186–1396) was too much under the influence of Byzantine ideas and forms of government to have any strong assembly of estates. Apart from a relatively small council of princely officials, there were from time to time large assemblies or *Sobore*; but they seem to have been notable for their activity as a kind of church synod, especially in the struggles against the Bogomil heresy. Perhaps like the *Sabori* of neighbouring Serbia, the assemblies of Bulgaria had a double root – the Old Slav popular assembly of warriors and the Christian provincial synod. It seems that in Serbia, for which there is better evidence, the popular assembly contracted into an assembly of nobles as the army of peasant foot-soldiers was superseded by the army of knightly horsemen. In the second half of the twelfth century, especially in the reign of Stefan Nemanya, the influence of Byzantine autocracy led to a further shrinking of the noble assembly into an advisory council of princely dignitaries. There were, to be sure, larger assemblies called *Sabori* during the late twelfth, the thirteenth and fourteenth centuries, more frequent and better reported than the *Sobore* of Bulgaria, and sometimes engaged in apparently important activities, such as the recognition of a ruler or (as in 1196) the formal renunciation of power of the ruler on his withdrawal to a monastery. Some important royal gifts of land were there solemnly ratified. The close relationship of Church and state led to the participation of *Sabori* in weighty matters of religion, such as the organization of the Church and the condemnation of heresy; the election and enthronement of the archbishop (later the patriarch) always took place in the context of a *Sabor*.

Phrased like this, the role of the Serbian *Sabor* can be made to appear important and independent. But it was in fact always very dependent on the king; it was he who decided if he would convoke it, he alone determined its business and determined who should be summoned to it. Courtiers and officials were prominent in its membership – the queen, the crown prince, the high dignitaries of the court, the governors of provinces, the archbishop or patriarch, the bishops, the abbots. It is true that a considerable number of the nobility, especially the high nobility, were summoned to the *Sabori*; but, as in Byzantium or seventeenth-century Russia, it was difficult to distinguish between officials and nobles. The high dignitaries were at the same time great nobles, and the upper nobility occupied the highest posts at court and in the provinces. In these circumstances it is not surprising that the functions of the *Sabori* were almost purely advisory (except in an interregnum or a revolutionary situation); nor shall we be astonished to find that they never developed a stable personnel or a firm organization. Some liberal-minded Serbian historians have patriotically supposed that eventually the *Sabor* would have developed into something more like a western parliament, if the Serbian state had not been overwhelmed by the terrible disasters of the Maritza (1371) and Kossovo (1389), which were to leave the Serbs under the Turkish yoke for the next half-millennium. This is nothing more than conjecture. The firm facts are that during the two centuries of the Serbian state the *Sabor* never gave any indication of acquiring the stability or the powers of the Estates in the realms of Latin Christendom.

If Serbia had survived as a state and had come under western influence, it is indeed plausible to suppose that the *Sabor* might have acquired some of the traits of a western parliament. We have an interesting example of such a development in the case of the Rumanian principalities of Wallachia and Moldavia. Though the Rumanians spoke a Latin language and were always to be proud of their connection with Rome, they received their Christianity and their basic culture from Byzantium. The Wallachian state began to consolidate itself in the late thirteenth century, when the cultural influence of Byzantium, exultant after the expulsion of the hated Latins from Constantinople, was still strong; and in the early years of the principality the influence of Byzantine autocracy was pronounced. But in 1352 Ludwig the Great of Hungary asserted his supremacy over Wallachia; and in 1418 the *voivode* or governor, Michael the Great of Wallachia, was defeated by the Turks. Thenceforward the Wallachians or Vlachs were either allies of Hungary or subjects of Turkey. It is not surprising that the influence of Hungarian society and institutions increased, nor that a *Sobor* should have developed with representative elements and, at times, considerable powers. The union of Wallachia and Transylvania in 1595, in order the more effectively to combat the Turks, was ratified by a *Sobor*, which insisted on guarantees for the liberties and privileges of the Wallachian clergy and nobility, and for the rights of its council of boyars, or 'barons'. In 1631 and again in 1669 assemblies of the Wallachian estates, backed by force, extorted important financial concessions from their princes, harassed at that time by Turkish financial demands, and by the fiscal instruments of the Turks, the Greek tax-collectors.

Moldavia was a later creation as a state than Wallachia, and was scarcely launched on its career before its *voivodes* became vassals of the kings of Poland, in the fifteenth century. In 1448 the prince of Moldavia and his boyars are recorded as doing homage to the king of Poland in a *Sejm* or parliament. In the early sixteenth century the Moldavian *voivode* Bogdan was forced to accept the suzerainty of the Sultan of Turkey. Thereafter until the extinction of the line of native princes in 1711, the Moldavian *voivodes* and nobles looked to support from Hungary or Poland against the Turks; and Hungarian and Polish influence became strong, both in society and government. Successive *voivodes* confirmed privileges of the powerful noble class, of the clergy, and even of the merchants. The pressure of the Poles and the demands of the sultans made life difficult for the *voivodes*, who were apt to suffer startling reversals of fortune. This gave great opportunity to the assembly of estates, which reached the point of

38

highest influence in the seventeenth century. Then they made and unmade princes and extorted concessions in return for support – concessions not only for the assembly but for the classes on whose support they counted, such as the hastening of legal enserfment of the peasantry. In all this they were much influenced by the example of the Polish parliament or *Sejm*, whose name they even sometimes adopted. After 1721 the Turks usually sold the governorship to the highest bidder, and under firm Turkish rule there was less scope for the exercise of power by the estates, which were, however, so firmly established in the tradition of the country that they continued to play a prominent part down to the constitutional reform of the Revolution of 1848.

MUSCOVITE RUSSIA AND THE ZEMSKI SOBOR

It is clear from the history of these Orthodox states of south-eastern Europe that in so far as they were inspired by Byzantine ideas and culture their larger assemblies were not parliaments in any western sense, and that in so far as they developed something like a parliament, as in the Rumanian principalities, it was under western influences. There remains, however, the problem of the greatest Orthodox state outside the Byzantine Empire – that of Muscovite Russia. This deserves some consideration, not only because it became powerful but because some Russian historians have seen in its history representative assemblies of some power. In Russian history, before the advent of avowedly western notions of democratic government in the nineteenth and twentieth centuries, there have been three types of 'popular assembly', of which we can quickly dismiss two. The earliest, before the days of the rise of Muscovy, was the *vece* or *vetche* (meaning 'conference' or 'discussion'), which flourished especially before the Mongol invasions, and afterwards in those towns free from Mongol rule, such as Novgorod and Pskov, until they in turn were conquered by Moscow. The *vetche* was not a representative assembly in the ordinary sense of the term, but a town's meeting, usually of the heads of free families. They were not summoned periodically even in towns where they were at one time powerful, as in Novgorod; they could at times act independently of the prince (notably in being summoned by a group of citizens without his assent), and they could and did take important decisions – the choice of ruler, the decision of peace or war, the imposition of taxes, the making of laws. Nevertheless, from what we know about them they appear a primitive institution, for which it is difficult to see a promising development in a more sophisticated society. They do not appear to have had any regular constitution, they were restricted to the bigger towns, and they were limited by the conditions of 'direct democracy' (e.g. the number of people in a crowd out of doors who can grasp what is taking place in a discussion when there are no mechanical aids such as loudspeakers). Their procedure, such as it was, appears to have been primitive. For example, there was a rule of unanimity, but this was not a decorous single-minded acclaim or a peaceful exercise of self-restraint. It was to be achieved, as several examples show, by the browbeating or bludgeoning of the minority by something like a riot into an enforced silence – the silence of death or unconsciousness. In any event the Grand Princes of Moscow, with their growing notions of Byzantine autocracy, had no use for the institution, and it disappeared promptly whenever they took a city. After 1510 there were no more *vetche* anywhere in the territory of pre-Mongol Russia.

The other examples of 'popular assemblies' before the twentieth century in Russia that do not claim much consideration are the legislative commissions of the eighteenth century. There seem to be four instances: under Catherine I, Peter II, Elizabeth and, most significantly, Catherine II. The first three commissions seem to have contained only a small number of representatives, summoned to give their advice on projects already prepared by commissions of officials. Under Catherine II representatives of the people were summoned for an important task – the preparation of a code of laws – and this time they were not simply advisers of officials but were themselves to form 'the Commission for the preparation of the project of the new Code'. The free population was widely represented, down to small free-holders, the number of deputies was large – 564 – and the duration of the assembly was long – one and a half years of 203 plenary sessions. Its information on the state of Russia was highly useful to the empress; but it was not conceived as anything but a consultative institution. Catherine's instruction, setting it up, made it quite clear that it did not limit the autocracy of the tsardom in the least.

So we come to the only type of pre-twentieth-century Russian assembly which has a claim to consideration as being in any way comparable to a western parliament – the *Zemski Sobor*, the 'council of all the land', meetings of which took place at irregular intervals in the sixteenth and seventeenth centuries. It is only for such assemblies in the seventeenth century that any serious comparison with the parliaments of the west can be attempted. There were several assemblies of the *Zemski Sobor* in the later sixteenth century – in 1549, 1550, 1566, 1584, and 1598 – but, except for the last, there is no real evidence that they were anything but assemblies of officials – lay officials such as the military leaders and the members of the council of boyars, and ecclesiastical officials such as the patriarch and bishops, archimandrites, abbots and archpriests, together with merchants administering the public finances. All this was pointed out by the great historian Klyuchevsky with moderation and learning more than sixty years ago. Most Soviet historians kept to the Klyuchevsky tradition; in 1958 Tikhomirov tried to oppose it but did so unconvincingly. His arguments were extremely indirect, such as 'the lively and patriotic character of speech of the merchants of Smolensk' at the *Sobor* of 1566. This assembly had been summoned by Ivan IV to inform him of the military and financial resources available to him for his war in Livonia, and officials could have given him this information just as well as elected deputies. This and the assembly of 1598 are the only ones of the sixteenth century for which we have any detailed information; and that of 1598 already reveals the breakdown of the conditions of the sixteenth-century summonses of the *Sobor*. They had been the instruments of the tsar; but now the last of the House of Rurik was dead, without an heir. In the interregnum Patriarch Iov called a *Sobor* to elect a new tsar; and to give this council the maximum authority, he summoned to it delegates of the common people. The strong and able Boris Godunov was chosen; but his election turned out to bring, not order, but the Time of Troubles. In the disintegration of government that followed in the next decade the officials lost something of their former authority, for there was no unchallenged tsar to back them. On the other hand it was necessary to form local militia to cope with the growing disorder and foreign intervention, and elected councils were formed in the towns and provinces to assure public order and organize national defence. This in turn strengthened the notion of taking important decisions with common consent. When Boris died in 1605, a *Sobor* containing delegates of the common people, as in 1598, was called to elect a successor. By 1611, when the Poles had taken Smolensk and occupied Moscow and the Swedes had captured Novgorod, when the murdered second false Dmitri had been succeeded in Pskov by a third pretender, it was clear to all that the country was falling to pieces and must have a tsar, if possible clearly accepted by all Russians.

When, in 1613, Moscow had been recovered from the Poles, the right moment seemed to have come; and the assembly to elect a tsar could, in the circumstances, not be limited, as in the sixteenth century, to officials. It must include elected representatives, especially as the provincial and town councils were in command of formidable armed forces. Hence the *Zemski Sobor* of 1613 was composed not only of office-holders, clerical and secular, but of elected representatives of provinces and towns; for since 1598 Russians had become used to the novelty of taking into account the opinions of the *miri* or local communities. The *Zemski Sobor* that called Michael Romanov to the tsardom not only contained important elective elements, but demanded a charter in which Michael promised to do nothing on his own initiative and to be always willing to resign all matters of administration to the boyars. The circumstances may well have seemed favourable for the development of the government on Polish lines. Michael was only a boy of sixteen and a gentle, timid one at that, reluctant to leave the monastery where he had taken refuge and to accept the tsardom. In the first years of his reign the work of government was therefore very much in the hands of the council of boyars, actively assisted by the *Zemski Sobor*, which helped the government in trying to restore order and raise revenue. In 1619 the government ordered the delegates to the *Sobor* to furnish reports and petitions of the grievances of the communities they represented, a feature that produced a still closer resemblance to a western parliament. To liberal-minded historians of the reign of Alexander II, like Sergeyevich and Latkin, the situation seemed full of promise for the development of representative government in Russia.

Like the reign of Alexander II, this situation after 1613 proved a false and fleeting dawn. One of the main reasons for Michael's election had been that he was the grand-nephew of the last tsar of the House of Rurik. There was a widespread feeling, enhanced by the terrible experiences of the Time of Troubles, that Russia's hope lay in the re-creation of a strong tsardom, based on hereditary right and tradition. The fearful devastations had not been favourable to the representation of peasants and merchants, for the widespread plundering had greatly accelerated the decline of the peasantry into serfdom

20 The proclamation in Red Square of the election of Michael Romanov by the *Zemski Sobor*, representing both officialdom and the people.

and the interruption of trade and burning of towns had ruined many merchants. The boyars looked to a strong tsardom to protect their positions against upstarts, and the new service nobility, the *dvoriane*, looked to a strong tsardom to guarantee their social status. Soon the *Sobor's* role was reduced to that of support for the government, to invest the government's decisions (especially in taxation and foreign policy) with the aura of popular approval. The messages of Michael (or of his advisers) to the *Sobor* sounded an increasingly imperious note. 'You have asked me to be tsar; now grant me the wherewithal to rule, and do not trouble me with over-much advice.' Increasingly in official documents Michael was entitled 'Autocrat'; and when his father Filaret returned to Russia from foreign imprisonment in 1619 and was elected Patriarch, he was determined to make a reality of his son's title as the only hope for peace and strong government in Russia. *Sobori* continued to be held, but the element of real election waned, the element of nomination increased, and the business came to be limited more and more to seeking support for moves in foreign

43

policy (such as attacks on Poland in 1621 and 1632) on which the government had already determined. At times the *Sobor* would venture on criticisms of the government, as in the celebrated meeting of 1642; but most of their criticisms clashed with those of other groups, and the government could afford to disregard such patent confusion. When Michael died, his son Alexis ascended the throne by hereditary right, without any *Sobor* being consulted.

The government had already forgotten that autocratic government would only be tolerated if it was associated with administrative honesty and reform. In the spring of 1648 the population of Moscow petitioned for the redress of grievances; when the government refused, the people rioted and the city was set ablaze. Terrified, Alexis not only sacrificed unpopular officials to be lynched by the mob, but promised to summon a truly elective *Zemski Sobor*, charged with no less a task than the compilation of a code of laws, 'so that men of all ranks in the Muscovite state, from the highest to the lowest, shall have justice equally in all matters'. The *Sobor* met in September 1648 and was for the first time organized into two chambers, an upper house of clergy and boyars, presided over by the tsar, and a lower one of elected deputies, who seem to have numbered about 350, elected by the gentry and leading merchants of districts all over Russia. This arrangement allowed the elected deputies to express their views without being overawed by the presence of the tsar and boyars; and the resulting code of nine hundred articles, completed by April 1649, seems to show plenty of evidence of the influence of the deputies' petitions. True, these deputies represented only the upper ranks of society, and this was the code which finally bound the peasants in legal serfdom to the landowners. Nevertheless, a supporter of parliaments from western Europe visiting Russia at this time might well have been impressed by the relatively broad representative character of this assembly and the influence that it had exerted in a really important matter.

For this very reason, the government was afraid that it might become dangerous. The tsar and his advisers were very disappointed when in 1650 a *Sobor*, with nation-wide election of deputies as in 1648, and meeting in two chambers, refused to back the government's wish to proclaim suzerainty over the Ukraine, with the war against Poland that that would involve. The government had to watch, in anger, as the *hetman* of the Cossacks was defeated by the Poles. By 1653 it was determined to act against Poland, but it wanted the appearance of national support. It therefore summoned a *Zemski Sobor* chosen largely by nomination and dominated by the army; the assembly dutifully accepted Russian suzerainty over the Ukraine, thereby involving Russia in the fateful war with Poland.

This was the last discussion of the government with any elected deputies that can properly be called a *Zemski Sobor*. After 1653 the government was content to take the advice of restricted social groups. Several such meetings were held to discuss social and administrative problems such as the high price of grain; and in 1662 all the groups present called for a *Zemski Sobor* on the ground that the real reason for the widespread distress, the debasement of the coinage, demanded a consultation with towns and men of every degree. But the government feared that a *Sobor* would give effective opposition to its monetary and social policies, and it turned a deaf ear. In 1681 the first minister, Prince Golitsyn, discussed plans of fiscal and military reform with elected delegates of gentry and merchants, and at about the same time a Church council was held. But all three assemblies were deliberately kept apart; the days of the *Zemski Sobor* were ended. Tsar Alexis, the son of a tsar who had enjoyed only limited power, was a fully autocratic ruler and held strongly to the old exalted view of the imperial authority. In his utterances we can hear again the echo of the Byzantine tradition of Ivan the Terrible. 'God hath blessed Us, the Tsar, and hath given unto Us to rule and to judge truly Our people.' The tsar and his ministers now had sure means of enforcing their will – a constantly expanding swarm of loyal bureaucrats and a trained regular army. The notion of consulting elected deputies, which had played such a striking role in the proclamation of Michael Romanov as tsar in 1613, quickly disappeared. When in 1682 the successor of Alexis, Tsar Theodore, died childless, there was no thought of summoning a duly elected *Zemski Sobor* as in 1613. The future Peter the Great was proclaimed by the Patriarch before a hastily assembled crowd in Red Square, Moscow.

The *Zemski Sobor* had come into existence in the late sixteenth century as a mere instrument of the government. The breakdown after 1598 of the tsarist autocracy, to which everyone in Russia had hitherto looked for orders, encouraged and indeed almost forced the growth throughout the provinces of elected assemblies, and from that fact the presence of elected deputies in the central assembly. But, when, after 1613, the greatest crisis of anarchy and foreign aggression was past and an undoubtedly legitimate tsar was placed on the throne, the *Sobor* was revealed as a plant without any firm roots in Russian conditions. The Byzantine tradition of the God-given authority of the ruler left no room for the political rights of social classes, secured in law and expressed in an elected assembly with powers of legislative initiative; and that autocratic tradition revived with great speed because it met the demands of the strongest forces in Russia at that time. In Russia, unlike the western countries, the power of the ruler had developed earlier and quicker than that of social estates, the most powerful of which, the service nobility, was in fact largely the result of state action and derived its inspiration and social status from tsarist power. The boyars were scarcely interested in the *Sobor*; they preferred to exercise power, if they could, through the longer-established boyars' council. After 1613 the *Sobor* quickly acquiesced in the role assigned to it by the government, that of acclaiming government proposals, providing the government with information and petitions, and giving a popular veneer to its policies, both home and foreign. Kabanov was probably right in the main (in spite of Keep's objections) in saying that the deputies on the whole found their duties burdensome, except at times of widespread excitement and unrest, as in 1648; and the peasantry, rapidly sinking into serfdom, were in no position to claim or even think about representation or political rights. The service nobility and the gentry might at times be restive about particular abuses of government or about specially unpopular ministers; but they were willing to back the tsardom in its broad lines of policy and were not prepared to support, against tsarist opposition, so alien an institution as a representative assembly insisting on rights and privileges.

So the *Zemski Sobor* as a representative institution survived barely half a century. It might not have merited so long a discussion in this context had it not been for the large claims sometimes made for it, or its potentialities. But on examination it appears not much more impressive than the Serbian *Sabor* as a representative assembly, by the standards of western Europe. There, too, in the seventeenth century absolutist tendencies were growing, but the absolutism was of a different kind and the powers of representative assemblies in various countries were still impressive. From 1652 onwards the Polish *Sejm* was practising the famous (or notorious) *liberum veto*, whereby a

21 Execution of King Charles I in 1649. In the mid-seventeenth century the powers of representative assemblies were considerable.

single member could not only thwart the proposal to which he objected, but also dissolve the *Sejm*. In Sweden Gustavus Adolphus had taken the *Riksdag* into partnership, keeping it informed of the political situation and of his aims and asking it for taxes and military forces; and his successors had continued his policy. In the Netherlands the States-General was the sovereign power and its members were addressed as 'Your High Mightinesses'; they had just defeated an attempt of William II to increase his power and after his death had abolished his office as *Stadhouder*. In Sicily (1636) the *Parlamento* had opposed an attempt to introduce obligatory military service for certain categories of persons as infringing the island's privileges; and the haughty Spanish monarchy had accepted the refusal. In England the Parliament had in the 1640s defeated the king in war and in 1649 had cut off his head. It does seem that representative assemblies, as vigorous, established and organized institutions, with important powers, were unique to western civilization. We are driven to ask why this should have been so, and how they came to be formed and developed.

47

luper mfcruu t comuftat c ualcc t   cs nob ucfugenu taue lj dici t lji noc
laxate funto's auc lj cunut ij fcruo t   tis quam totum tcmp qr unimus
clamalat uoc magna dicctcs un   tc tia. ui crgo quu tucoo duit dic tom
dicunus tc rpc fuu dci unu lj dignat   lju rpi licuut prte au fcas i fcta fclou

22 The orb, the sceptre and the holy oil – symbols of a Christian coronation.

In one form or another the summoning of Estates was an aspect of government, and in medieval Europe government was normally in the hands of a king. Medieval traditions of kingship had arisen in the setting of invasions and conquests by Germanic tribes and war-bands. The earliest descriptions of the Germanic peoples come from Romans who may have seen in these little-known tribes what they wanted to see, or at least have interpreted their institutions in the light of those of Roman society. It seems certain, however, that the Germanic leaders were expected to be successful in warfare, to display warlike virtues such as courage and fortitude, and to be generous to their followers if the latter proved themselves brave and loyal in their support. Tacitus did not expect the war-leader to be necessarily a king; and some of the German tribes of the fourth and fifth centuries appear to have managed without kings. It is also noteworthy that Tacitus, to whom the Roman tradition of the sacral functions of primitive kings must have been very familiar, pictures the Germanic king as more of a tribal leader than a priest. He may have been wrong; but it scarcely matters for our purpose, for the period of Germanic settlement in the lands that had formerly been part of the Roman Empire of the west wrought a tremendous change in the institution of Germanic kingship. For one thing, the opportunities of conquest helped the successful war-leader to emphasize his role as the *kuning* or kinnish man, head of the tribe (real or imagined). By the same process he emphasized his sacral character; he was the man who brought luck to his people and linked them with their past. He may have owed his pre-eminence to his skill and fortune in war and not to royal ancestry, but he had been successful, and to an unusual degree it was at this point the successful men who made the history.

There was another feature of the conquests that enhanced the position of the king. They brought the Germanic peoples much more intimately into contact with the culture of Rome, which by the fourth century had made its momentous fusion with the Christian religion.

One after another the Germanic peoples were converted to Christianity, first of the Arian and then of the Catholic variety. With Christianity came a literate priesthood which, if the king would co-operate, was glad to emphasize the authority of a ruler who could bring the peace within which the new faith could best be propagated, and the patronage with which it could be endowed. Literacy itself could be of service to the king by recording the outstanding deeds (whether real or fictitious) of his ancestors and the distinction of his genealogy. It is a curious fact that we owe to Christian chroniclers the records of genealogies that are magical, like that of the Merovingians whose ancestor Merovech was sired by a sea-beast, part bull, part man, or of genealogies that are clearly pagan, like the claims of various English dynasties to be descended from the god Woden. But the Christian faith had much more solid gifts for kingship than this. It brought memories of imperial Rome, and of emperors who had great power and even greater *auctoritas*.

Perhaps of even larger consequence in the circumstances was the example of the Old Testament kings; for, whether they were good, bad or indifferent in character, their authority clearly came from God, and their authority was a foreshadowing of the kingship of Christ. Bede's *Ecclesiastical History*, for example, which wielded tremendous influence (with kings among others – Coelwulf and Offa and Alfred had copies), had a great deal to say about kings; for Bede knew that in the circumstances of his time the leadership of kings (and sometimes queens) could be crucial in bringing people to the true faith and defending them in it from pagan assault. Kings like Edwin and Oswald could die as Christian champions and be revered as Christian martyrs.

Furthermore, the divine foundations of Christian kingship were soon to be given symbolic recognition in the initiation ceremony of the ruler. Instead of the symbols of the warrior – the raising on a shield to the shouts of the assembled host – or the symbols of the pagan magician – the seating on a stone of destiny – the new king was now to be crowned in a Christian ceremony, clothed in garments suggestive of those of a bishop, and (in the lands of the strongest kingship, like France and England) to be anointed like Solomon of old. In favourable circumstances the apotheosis of kingship could go far. In the late tenth century King Edgar could be compared in the *Regularis Concordia*, a work inspired by Benedictine bishops and abbots, to the Good Shepherd himself.

But along with Christian enhancement of royal authority went Christian insistence on the duties and limitations of kingship. Kings were appointed by God, it was true – but only as a means to an end, the furthering of right and justice. As St Isidore of Seville had said in a famous and influential exposition of kingship, a king who does not rule rightly is not a king but a tyrant. The king must show *pietas*, which was not only personal but involved the protection of doctrine, morals, the churches and all their officers and possessions. He must also uphold *justitia*, which involved not only the observance of divine law (as expounded by the Church) but the maintenance of all good custom and all just rights. It was generally held that these rights and customs included the right of the great men of the realm to be consulted about matters of policy and justice, and of all men (or their representatives) to be consulted before any of their wealth could be taken (otherwise than by custom) on any plea of royal necessity.

The stress on the duties of kingship was increased by the development in the Church of the Gregorian reform movement of the eleventh and twelfth centuries. The kingdom of God was to be sought by the development of a purified, disciplined hierarchy of clergy which would rule the Church under the direction of Christ's Vicar, the pope; and for the service of God even kings must learn that they were subject to the teaching and, if need be, the correction of the pope and even of the bishops in the exercise of their royal office. For kings, like their subjects, stood in need of salvation, of which the Church held the keys; and if it was true that kings ruled by the grace of God, it was also true that they might fall into moral disgrace, of which the precise gravity would be determined by the clergy, especially the pope.

Kings might and did object to the humiliating implications of this view; and some of them, especially the kings of France and England, managed to put up a considerable resistance to many of those implications. But even kings of France and England had to submit sometimes to papal censures; and all kings were put on the defensive by the development of this High Church doctrine and its popularity (growing for several generations) with educated men. Kings had to be more careful in the exercise of their office, more concerned to be seen to observe law and custom. Their literate advisers were all clerics, who, devoted as they might be to their royal masters, could not remain oblivious to the persuasive High Church doctrines that were gaining

23 *(Left)* The king as judge, having his authority from God. A twelfth-century MS. shows Solomon, supported by the estates and orders; the scroll in his hands quotes from Proverbs 20 on the wickedness of false weights, and from the Book of Wisdom, 'Love justice, ye who judge the earth'.

24 *(Opposite)* Raising the crowned monarch on a shield – symbol of the warrior king.

so much influence in the Church in which they might well hold office as bishops or archdeacons. So they were likely, as royal counsellors, to emphasize to the king the duties of his office and to persuade him to follow set rules.

By the twelfth and thirteenth centuries there were, in many kingdoms of western Christendom, other reasons for the ruler to observe due forms – especially in the consultation of important social groups. For one thing, the increasing stability of western Europe, its new-found freedom from invasions that might ruin its culture or its economic viability, the recovery of so much of the knowledge of the Graeco-Roman world and the Near East, the heightened sense of law and logic fostered by recent controversies between papacy and empire, all worked together to make possible more effective administration of kingdoms and bolder enterprises. In the more developed kingdoms of the west the king now had better means of surveying his finances, more effective methods of doing and recording his secretarial work, his official acts, his commands, more ways, both persuasive and forceful, of offering and enforcing royal justice and order. The total effect was to increase the power and self-confidence of the king, who was enabled to think of operating on a much bigger scale

than his predecessors had commonly been able to do. The Germanic tradition of the king as successful war-leader was still very potent, and the increased royal power was especially used to indulge in bigger wars – either against the infidel or the heathen in the form of crusades, or against fellow Christians in the less respectable but compelling cause of territorial aggrandizement. For a peculiar feature of western culture was that it never became united in a universal empire which could have imposed an authoritarian rule over western Europe. Instead there were always to be a number of states struggling with each other for increased power and larger territories.

But though the king's might was now commonly big enough to encourage him to contemplate such enterprises, his authority was not yet strong enough for him to embark on them without the conscious consent of socially important groups in his kingdom. In part this rested on military necessity; there was as yet no bureaucratic machinery capable of organizing the whole of an adequate royal army through paid administrators alone. Hence the most effective part of the army had to be in the form of baronial contingents, led by nobles who were used to exercising social, economic, and political leadership. To ignore the opinions of such men in the formulation of

53

policy would be an obvious folly. Such practical considerations were powerfully reinforced by the influence of ideas. The ancient Germanic tradition that the war-leader should take the advice of his followers before going into action was now reinforced by the teaching of the Church that the good king took the advice of his leading men. Indeed it was commonly thought that this was one of the features which distinguished a king from a tyrant. The increasing tendency to analyse and define encouraged greater awareness of the claims of great ecclesiastics and great landowners (whether as feudal vassals in the more developed lands of the west or on more general grounds in the less feudalized lands of central Europe and Scandinavia) to advise the king.

This attitude of mind affected the interpretation of the revived Roman law, which was so much admired. It might be expected that the influence of Roman law, with its insistence on the ruler as law-giver, would enhance the authority of the king; and so in many ways it did. But in the mood of the late twelfth and the thirteenth centuries emphasis was laid on the fact that the imperial right to enact law was originally founded on a grant from the people; and in thirteenth-century conditions the people were (at any rate outside northern Italy) commonly held to be represented by the great clerics and nobles. So though the law-giver might indeed be the king, the laws he made would be all the more firmly grounded if he made them after consultation with his leading men.

Representation was a crucial ingredient in the development of parliamentary institutions. Before the middle of the eleventh century, when the reform movement in the Church began to make an impact on political thinking, kings in the more developed realms had often summoned councils to discuss important questions – matters of peace or war, the conclusion of an important alliance or marriage, the determining of a disputed succession, even the making of laws. But this was done on a customary basis; and from the standpoint of the thirteenth century the lack of coherent principle was shown by the transaction of ecclesiastical and royal business in the same assembly, so that it is often hard to say, regarding these early meetings, whether they were Church synods or royal councils. The eleventh-century Church reform movement and the twelfth-century renaissance not only made it seem a scandal for measures affecting the government of the Church or the upholding of the faith to be dealt with in royal

25 An eleventh-century Anglo-Saxon king with his council or *Witenagemot* of princes, nobles and ecclesiastics. The king in council had the duty of upholding the law, even to passing sentences of death.

councils; they encouraged a taste for definition and a self-awareness that were to be fertile in unforeseen consequences.

One result, powerfully reinforced by the social conditions of the age, promoted the notion of community – the community or *universitas* not only of closely knit and visible groups such as chartered towns, or academic bodies of masters or students, but wider social groups such as the nobility or the clergy (who were now conceived to have rights and duties in common), or even wider and vaguer groups such as the community of a province or a realm. In the thirteenth century, even in a country with a very powerful and old-established monarchy such as England, where the king insisted on consulting his great men as individuals, the magnates and prelates increasingly insisted on their role as virtual representatives of the rest of the nobility and the clergy and even of the community of the realm. And so there was not only a stress on the obligation of the ruler to his subjects – *Sicut subditus domino, ita dominus subdito tenetur*, as Matthew Paris neatly expressed it – but a stress on the obligation of the king to consult the important communities in his realm on matters for which custom required it. The pressure of the expanding monarchies alarmed those groups which were specially powerful and yet felt particularly threatened into drawing together into associations for self-defence. For in thirteenth- and fourteenth-century western Europe threatened groups could not escape growing government pressure by wholesale emigration. The famous German expansion beyond the Elbe was not on a big enough scale to enfeeble the urge towards the kind of defensive solidarity of nobles, clergy, and towns which spread throughout Latin Christendom.

Custom might demand not only the advice but the consent of the subjects if their active participation was required in a royal act which their obligations to the king did not bind them to accept without question. If the king wished nobles to fight for him in an area outside their normal obligation, or to fight for him without his personal leadership, nobles were prone to say that their consent must be obtained, as they said in the England of King John and King Edward I. And if the king wished to take his subjects' money in extraordinary aids, other than for urgent military need to defend the realm, he must gain their permission. In a society where the higher clergy and the barons formed the ruling class, it was possible to regard them as the virtual representatives of the community of the realm for this purpose as well; but as the towns developed both in self-consciousness as closely knit communities and also as centres of wealth, it came to seem unrealistic for the higher clergy and the nobles to speak for the towns in matters of taxation.

The late twelfth and the thirteenth centuries were not only a time when kingdoms were becoming better organized and more capable of military adventure, but also a time when the cost of warfare was rising, from the wages paid to knights to the cost of the armour and the horses they used. So kings began to summon the leading towns of their realms to their councils. This encouraged the idea of representation. Archbishops, bishops and abbots might be thought to represent the clergy in virtue of their high offices; the greatest nobles might be held to represent the rest in virtue of their high rank. But townsmen had to give (whether voluntarily or under duress) a mandate to deputies who would represent them in the royal assembly. Some have seen in the practice of representation a following of the example of representation within the Church, for instance in the constitution of general councils and provincial councils, and in the government of newer religious orders such as the Dominicans. Others have thought that it arose as a commonsense solution to the problem of getting a coherent answer from an active community on whom a demand was made from outside. There was probably an element of both factors in varying proportions at different times in different places; what is clear is that representation on the scale that was now beginning had never, so far as we know, been used as an instrument of government in any previous culture.

If the king was strong enough, he insisted that the representatives should have full power to agree on behalf of their constituents to whatever should be decided at the assembly by common consent, as both Roman law and canon law prescribed. Edward I of England saw to it that the representative knights and burgesses had such plenipotentiary powers, at any rate in his later Parliaments; this was the rule henceforth in England, probably to the discontent of representatives and their constituents in the early days, but to the advantage of representatives in later centuries, when they could claim to speak for the people of England. In some other countries, for example Castile and, later, the Netherlands, the ruler was not strong enough to insist on this. In Castile, for instance, every city represented in the *Cortes* gave its *procuradores* letters of instruction called *poderes*, from which the *procuradores* were forbidden to deviate in the slightest; on any doubtful matter they were to refer back for fresh instructions.

But even if the representatives had only a limited mandate, their appearance in the royal assembly was of crucial importance. It emphasized the willingness of the king to seek advice and consent, on matters of common concern, from those who could claim to speak for wide but coherent groups of his subjects. Even if elected representatives were absent from one of these early assemblies, the notion of representation encouraged contemporary writers to make a distinction between those council meetings of the king which dealt with routine or private matters and those council meetings which acted as public deliberative assemblies to treat with the king on matters of common concern. In such sessions, often called *colloquia* or *parlamenta* or *curiae* or the vernacular equivalents of these, such as *parlements* or *parlamenti* or *cortes*, the higher clergy and the nobles now assumed the role of speaking for their group or estate, or even of speaking for the community of the realm as a whole. In England, for example, contemporary chroniclers of Edward I's time were apt to refer to 'parlements' if the king and his continual councillors consulted members of the higher clergy and the nobility on the affairs of the realm, even if the elected representatives were not there. But, as in other countries, this was a transitional stage, and in the fourteenth century elected representatives became an integral part of the English Parliament.

III THE EMERGENCE AND DEVELOPMENT OF PARLIAMENTS IN WESTERN EUROPE

THE SPANISH CORTES

England was not the first country in which a parliament emerged. This happened in the kingdoms of Leon and Castile. Spanish historians of previous generations, eager to claim as great an antiquity as possible for Spanish institutions, sought to trace the origins of the *Cortes* in the councils of Visigothic Spain of the seventh and eighth centuries. It is possible to see a tenuous connection; but it would be equally valid to trace the origins of the English Parliament or the French Estates-General back to the councils of Anglo-Saxon England or Merovingian Gaul. More relevant are the social and constitutional conditions of Leon and Castile in the twelfth century. Their kings were insecure rulers of small and turbulent kingdoms. The constant struggles against the Moors had fostered both the importance and the insubordination of the warrior aristocracy, and emphasized the duty of the king to make ceaseless war against the infidel. Successful war was almost a necessity for the king, not only to maintain his prestige but to provide territorial rewards for a land-hungry aristocracy; yet warfare on this scale was a serious drain on his resources. The constant border wars caused all towns to be fortresses, and their citizens to be trained to arms and granted special privileges to encourage them to resist the Moor. Townsmen too, therefore, had a spirit of independence, turbulence, and dignity. The king, in need of political and military aid and money, early looked to the towns for help in these matters and for support against the unruly aristocracy.

In the first *concilio* of Leon to which representatives of towns were summoned, that of 1188, King Alfonso IX of Leon made concessions which seem to indicate an alliance between the clergy, aristocracy, and towns. For example, he promised that he would consult the bishops, nobles, and 'good men' (*hombres buenos*) on matters of peace and war, and that the three estates (*brazos*) would be summoned to future meetings of the *Cortes*. But in future meetings the king was on

26 The coronation of Alexander I, King of Poland, in December 1501. In his reign the power of the *Sejm* was recognized and defined in the Constitution of Radom, *Nihil Novi* (May 1505).

many occasions to rely on the towns against troublesome nobles. It is likely that this innovation in Leon influenced the sister kingdom of Castile, with which it was soon to be united. When an important meeting took place in Castile in 1188, at Carrión, to accept the marriage contract between the Infanta Berenguela and the son of the Emperor Frederick Barbarossa, besides higher clergy and lay lords there were summoned the *majores* (governors) of forty-eight cities. But unlike the *Cortes* of Leon in the same year, there is no evidence that the assembly of Carrión had any elected representatives of towns. It is not certain that elected representatives of Castilian towns were summoned until the union of the two *Cortes* in 1250.

By that time the *Cortes* had become an established institution of the kingdom of Leon and Castile, and it was accepted that it should be composed of three estates – clergy, nobles, and towns. Its importance continued to grow and by the end of the fourteenth century its powers were in many respects impressive. The urban representatives, the *procuradores*, were given careful letters of instruction by which they were strictly bound; this strengthened their hands in relation to the king, for unusual and unwelcome royal demands could be delayed and even at times eroded or evaded by a counter-move, the *procuradores* insisting that they must consult their constituents – a process that could take much time and lead to bargaining.

The control of the towns over their *procuradores* was reinforced until 1422 by the fact that it was the towns which paid their wages and expenses to attend the *Cortes*; in that year King Juan II promised to pay these sums instead. Later, this was to open the door to dangerous royal influence over the town *procuradores* and a deliberate limitation of their number in the interests of economy, but at the time it was simply a reflection of the important advances they had gained in the fourteenth century, including the right to complete freedom of speech in the *Cortes* and to liberty from arrest during its sessions.

By the fourteenth century the king had conceded considerable powers to the *Cortes* as a whole. Firstly, it was repeatedly reaffirmed that the king could not levy extraordinary taxes without an explicit grant from the *Cortes*. Towards the end of the century the *Cortes* several times insisted on an audit of the expenditure it had authorized, and three times it secured a partial appropriation of the grant. Secondly, it had the right to present petitions which, if conceded, became the

27 Battle scene from the Reconquest. Ceaseless warfare against the Moors strengthened the hands of the nobility as against the king.

basis of laws; these petitions spanned a very wide range of topics. And finally, the *Cortes* had to be consulted in all matters of importance for the welfare of the realm; when a new king ascended the throne, it was customary for him to swear in the presence of the *Cortes* to observe the laws; and when the heir was a minor the *Cortes* exercised considerable power over the regency.

All this looks impressive; but there were serious flaws in the role of the *Cortes*, defects which were later to prove its undoing. Firstly, the clergy and nobles were generally exempt from taxation, so that the *procuradores* could not look to them for any support in any financial argument with the Crown. Secondly, the kings never gave up their claim that certain taxes (especially the *alcabala*, or tax on sales) were not 'extraordinary', and this could be used to turn the flank of the third estate if it insisted on its control of taxation. Thirdly, the *Cortes* never managed to turn its right of petitioning into a right of sharing

61

in law-making. These weaknesses were due to various factors. The *Cortes* never succeeded in making taxes dependent on redress of grievances; it never developed an effective procedure; and, above all, it was so disunited that when, in the sixteenth century, the Crown became strong, it could divide and rule. Not only did the clergy and nobles despise the townsmen, and the townsmen envy the other two estates; they quarrelled among themselves. For example, from 1348 to 1570 there was a bitter struggle between Toledo and Burgos for precedence; the disputants often almost came to blows, and in 1506 they shouted at each other so loud and long that no one could understand a word and the session was disrupted. And the Crown always retained some valuable prerogatives. No one gained a right to a permanent summons to the *Cortes*. The greatest prelates and nobles might expect to receive a summons, but even their presence depended on the king's pleasure. The number of towns represented declined so rapidly from the fourteenth century onwards that the Catholic kings tried to stabilize the figure at eighteen. And the Crown always insisted on keeping the right to decide when a meeting should be summoned. Some kings, like Fernando IV and Juan I, summoned a meeting every year; others let ten years elapse without a session of the *Cortes*.

The *Cortes* of Aragon developed later than that of Castile, but its privileges became more impressive. When it reached its final frontiers under Jaime I (1213–76), 'the Conqueror', the kingdom of Aragon was really a federation of three regions, the differences between which led to the establishment of a separate *Cortes* for each. The mountainous original kingdom of Aragon had been united in 1137 by a marriage to the trading country of Catalonia; and in 1238 Jaime I of Aragon-Catalonia had conquered the province of Valencia, with its mixed population of Christians, Moors, and Jews. The *Cortes* of Old Aragon began to form in the thirteenth century when representatives of towns were summoned to councils of nobles; the clergy were unaccountably absent until the latter half of the century, and did not attend in force until 1301. But by that time the membership of the clerical estate was rapidly hardening into certainty, as was that of the estate of nobles (*brazo noble*), so that the Crown had far less room for manipulating the attendance of the great men of the realm than in Castile. Membership of the *brazo noble* was greatly prized, for it was the hallmark of one's inclusion in the ranks of the

28 Jaime I presiding over the *Cortes* of Catalonia, one of the three regions of his kingdom of Aragon.

higher aristocracy; the lesser nobles and gentry were organized in a separate estate or *brazo de caballeros*.

In contrast to Castile it was legally stipulated that the *Cortes* of Aragon should meet periodically – after 1307 every two years. It is true that this rule was not strictly observed, but by this time there was in existence a powerful official called the *justicia de Aragón*, whose business it was to safeguard the rights of the *Cortes*, whether it was in session or not.

By the fourteenth century the powers of the Aragonese *Cortes* were impressive. Its agreement was essential for the passing of all legislation; the king could not enact laws without it. Some writers have thought it a miracle that any law was made in Aragon, for in theory a unanimous vote in each of the four *brazos* was necessary for the validation of any statute. The *Cortes* showed, however, much practical sense by often appointing by majority vote a committee of four or more members of each *brazo*, with full powers to act, so circumventing the unanimity rule. The opening formula of Aragonese laws was nevertheless impressive: 'El señor Rey de voluntad de la Corte estatuesce y ordena' ('Our lord the king, with the consent of the Cortes, establishes and ordains'). Furthermore, it was the rule in Aragon that all extraordinary revenue for the king could be levied only with the consent of the *Cortes*. Without its approval no new tax could be raised, nor could the mode of collection or the rate of any old one be changed.

When the *Cortes* was not in session, a committee chosen by it and called the *diputación permanente* had the duty of watching over the proper observance of the laws and the honest administration of the public funds. The *Cortes* had other important functions. It discussed questions of peace and war, and ratified treaties; it sometimes nominated ambassadors; it had sole control of naturalization; it recognized the new king and received from him an oath to keep all the laws. Along with the *justicia* it could investigate all allegations of breaches of the law by officials or even by the king himself, at the expense of any individual or any group of persons, and it could demand that justice be done.

The *Cortes* of Catalonia differed somewhat in organization from the *Cortes* of Aragon, but its power in the fourteenth and fifteenth centuries was equally striking. The third estate appeared in the Catalonian *Cortes* in 1218, at Villafranca; but the *Cortes* was not fully established until 1283, when Pedro III issued a constitution promising to summon once a year in Catalonia an assembly of nobles, clergy and townsmen, to discuss the affairs of the realm, unless he was prevented by urgent necessity. The Catalonian *Cortes* was more normal in having three estates, of clergy, nobles, and towns; but the estate of towns resembled that of Aragon in having one town which dominated the others and was resented by them – Barcelona in Catalonia, Saragossa in Aragon. There was no *justicia*, as in Aragon, but there was a similar degree of control over legislation, finance, administration, and policy; and here, too, committees of the *Cortes* could exercise great powers over royal officials and the way they carried out the laws. The *Cortes* itself exercised minute control over the qualifications of its members; and at the end of every session the king had to swear to observe all the acts of the *Cortes* before he was granted the *donativo* or tax. Only the estate of nobles had a rule of unanimity; and this made procedure smoother than in Aragon.

In this as in other respects the *Cortes* of Valencia resembled closely that of Catalonia. The rule demanding unanimity among the nobles caused much trouble; and in heated moments it could lead to a dissentient being thrown out, so that unanimity could be achieved. The dominance of Valencia in the estate of towns or *brazo real* was even greater than that of Barcelona or Saragossa in their estates; Valencia claimed to represent half the *brazo real*, regardless of how many other towns sent representatives. Another peculiar custom of Valencia was the claim that each estate could continue to meet after the *Cortes* had been dissolved, in order to devise and present petitions to the Crown. Like the *Cortes* of Aragon and Catalonia, the *Cortes* of Valencia had the right to appoint a *diputación general* to watch over the privileges of the estates and the laws of the realm between sessions of the *Cortes*.

The extensive powers of the *Cortes* of the kingdom of Aragon are in large measure a reflection of the weak position of its kings in relation to the governing social groups, of the strains on the resources of the monarchs through foreign adventures, and of jealously guarded local particularisms. For example, towards the end of the thirteenth century Alfonso III was much concerned with trying to extricate himself from the conflict with France and the pope over the Aragonese conquest of Sicily from the French prince Charles of Anjou; and the nobles of Aragon took advantage of his difficulties to extort from him the *Privilegio de la Unión* in 1287, in which the king undertook not to kill any noble or representative in the *Cortes*, and to recognize the authority of the *justicia*.

The desire to protect local rights and class privileges can also be seen in the development of the *Cortes* of Navarre and Portugal. Their composition and privileges were ill defined by Aragonese standards; but they exercised a strict control over the grant of taxes to the Crown, they watched with jealous eyes any royal attempt to change or defy the laws without their consent, and yet they sprang to the aid of the monarchy if they felt that the independence of Portugal or Navarre was threatened. In the fifteenth century the turbulence of the nobility in Portugal, as in Castile, became so great as to lead to a reaction among the towns and clergy in favour of the Crown, and so to a fatal weakness in the power of the *Cortes* in those two countries; but in Navarre the *Cortes* survived until 1828.

The multiplicity and variety of *Cortes* in the Iberian peninsula sprang from the strong particularism of its regions. In France, too, this was an innate feature and, so far as its representative assemblies went, had similar consequences. The kings of France, since at least the beginning of the Capetian dynasty, had from time to time summoned great assemblies for wide areas of the realm, and these slowly led to meetings of Estates-General for the whole country. Hugh Capet had been raised to the throne by election. He and his successors depended on the support of the Church and the great feudatories and found it politic to consult their leading vassals on important questions. The kings tried to avoid opposition by summoning these large assemblies only to give approval to the royal will. But from the late twelfth century the monarchy was rapidly gathering both power and prestige, and kings like St Louis felt strong enough to summon great assemblies of ecclesiastics and nobles not only to gain their acclamation for royal acts, but to seek their advice. In the thirteenth century the towns were quickly rising in wealth and organization, and St Louis summoned representatives of the towns as well if he thought that the matter in hand was one on which the advice of burgesses would be useful – for example a question of trade or the exchange rates of the depreciating coinage. These practices were continued by his successors; in the assemblies of Bourges in 1283 and Paris in 1284, for example, the prelates and barons discussed at length the proposals of the pope for a crusade against Aragon because of the Sicilian Vespers of 1282 and their aftermath.

There were thus precedents for Philip the Fair to follow, after he became King in 1285, if he wished to seek widely based advice or gain general approbation for his policies. In 1302 he needed to do this in order to counter the effects of Pope Boniface VIII's bitter denunciations of his government in the bull *Ausculta fili*. In April 1302 Philip summoned to Paris a great assembly of prelates, barons, and burgesses, who were asked for advice and support by the king's minister, Pierre Flote, in the king's dispute with the pope. Admittedly this assembly was stage-managed and given no real initiative; admittedly it was not called an Estates-General. But it is hard to deny it a special place in the evolution of that institution, for it seems (if only for the king's propagandist purposes) to have been a fuller consultation of the French nation than any that had yet been attempted.

29 An effigy of Philip the Fair from the church of St Denis, Paris.

Great assemblies of the three estates continued to be summoned by Philip the Fair and his successors. We are usually not informed from what areas of the kingdom they were drawn in the early fourteenth century, but by the middle of the century it had become the custom to summon an Estates-General for the north of France, the Langue d'Oïl, and another for southern France, the Langue d'Oc. This was because of the size of the kingdom and the difficulty, for a large number of people, of travel to some central point, such as Paris, and also because the king's power over the more distant provinces had only recently become effective. Frenchmen in the south did not as yet feel sufficient solidarity with those of the north to wish to be bound by the decisions of a common assembly. The king for his part wanted the most effective form of assembly, and until the reign of Charles VII the Crown was usually content to summon separate Estates-General for Langue d'Oïl, Langue d'Oc, and Dauphiné. A major consideration

67

was to gain consent to the taxes that the monarchy must have for its bigger aims and larger expenditure; and if such grants could best be obtained from regional or local assemblies, it was pointless to make reluctant deputies travel long distances to meet other representatives with whom they might not work easily, or possibly to make trouble for the government by presenting far-reaching demands.

Even the policy of summoning an Estates-General for the Langue d'Oïl received a rude check from the monarchy's experiences of 1355 and 1356. The military disasters of those years, culminating in the capture of King John at the Battle of Poitiers, encouraged the Estates-General of the Langue d'Oïl, meeting at Paris, to make great demands for control of the government. Led by the third estate, and within that estate by Etienne Marcel, provost of the merchants of Paris, they demanded in 1355 the collection and spending of the taxes they voted by elected tax-gatherers under the estates' supervision; then,

30 *(Opposite)* The capture of King John of France at Poitiers left the monarchy in a weak position, forcing the Dauphin to make temporary concessions to the Estates-General.

31 The murder of Etienne Marcel: the leader of the third estate in its demands for increased control was a victim of the reaction against the peasants' revolt.

after Poitiers in 1356, they demanded the punishment of evil counsellors and the election by themselves of a council of state to govern the kingdom. The Dauphin, as regent for his captive father, had to make temporary concessions to gain time; but he was helped by the hostility of the nobles and clergy to the pretensions of Marcel and the third estate, and by the fears aroused among the upper classes by a formidable peasants' revolt, the Jacquerie. A reaction set in, Marcel was murdered, his supporters were executed, and the monarchy was restored. The third estate was composed of deputies of towns; it did not represent the mass of the people and had no authority with them, whereas the monarchy was the rallying-point for Frenchmen. For the next two generations the kings of France and their advisers tried to avoid summoning the Estates of Langue d'Oïl. No tradition of regular summons had been established, and it was the king who determined the object of the meeting in the letter of convocation.

The estates did not participate in legislation; they could only petition; and as for the granting of taxes, if that could be achieved in other ways, most of the provinces would be glad to be spared the expense and trouble of having to send deputies to Paris or some other central point.

In the forlorn earlier years of Charles VII, when by the Treaty of Troyes his own father and mother had willed the crown of France away to the king of England, Charles tried to rally support by holding meetings of the Estates-General of the Langue d'Oïl, and even Estates-General for the whole realm. But after nineteen years of effort he abandoned the use of large representative assemblies. The people of the outlying provinces disliked them; they had great difficulty in agreeing on taxation; and they presented a potentially dangerous and always disagreeable collection of grievances against the royal administrators.

After 1440 Charles gave up the attempt to use the Estates-General for consent to taxation; if such consent were needed, he would go direct to each province and town for help. No meeting of the Estates-General was held thereafter until 1468, when Louis XI wanted to harness public opinion to his purpose of depriving his brother of the dangerous position of Duke of Normandy. He managed the assembly well and got it to make just the recommendations he wanted, but he did not risk another meeting. The next time that the Estates-General was summoned was in the reaction after his death, when the regents for the boy king Charles VIII felt it politic to consider complaints against the government of Louis XI. The greatest danger was from the nobility, and it was perhaps to reduce their influence that the government ordered that in every *bailliage* or *sénéchaussée* the three estates should meet and jointly elect representatives of each. In some regions, however, the nobles and clergy insisted on choosing their own deputies, and some of the bishops demanded a personal right to attend. These signs of divisions between the estates were reinforced by stronger evidence of cleavage within estates. When the Estates-General had been induced to make a grant of 1,500,000 livres, there were vigorous protests about the allotment of the tax between the various provinces. This caused so much bad blood that the government thought it safe to order a dissolution. The unwieldy Estates-General was not to meet again until 1560.

This does not mean that there was no consultation of large or representative bodies for over seventy years. It means that the kings of France were confirmed in their view that it was better to deal with smaller assemblies, whether it was with national assemblies of nominated members of the aristocracy, the clergy, the lawyers, and officials, or with provincial Estates. The latter had evolved in the fourteenth century, possibly from varying origins such as feudal courts of barons and clergy or regional assemblies of differing social orders, in response to royal demands, especially for taxation. Such an arrangement had great mutual advantages. The king or his officials could talk directly to local notables or deputies who knew the area, its feelings and customs, and its capacity to pay; the local assembly could defend the privileges of that region and its leading groups, and present *cahiers* of requests and grievances related to local needs and aspirations. So provincial and regional Estates developed all over France; and though they soon wilted and died in central France, where the particularism and sense of local identity was not enough to keep them going through difficulties, in many of the outlying provinces of France they had become established institutions by the end of the fourteenth century. By the end of the fifteenth century their position was becoming entrenched, especially in provinces which had had a tradition of semi-independence of the Crown, such as Normandy, Languedoc, Dauphiné, Burgundy, Provence, and Brittany. They were even prepared to assert their rights against the Estates-General; in 1484, after the meeting of the Estates-General at Tours, the government had to go to the Estates of Dauphiné, Burgundy, Normandy, and Languedoc, to get their consent to bear the share of the tax voted by the deputies at Tours.

Unlike the Estates-General, the well-established provincial Estates were summoned regularly, according to the custom of the provinces, whether every year or every two or three years. Generally speaking, they began with a personal summons to the clergy holding the principal offices, and the nobles holding the most important lordships, together with deputies of towns. But by the sixteenth century local variations had arisen. There were no clergy in the Estates of Normandy or Brittany, and frequently none in Provence, very few nobles in the Estates of Languedoc, and neither clergy nor nobles in the Estates of Auvergne. On the other hand, where the two premier orders continued to sit, their representation became more important; in Brittany all nobles eventually gained the right to attend the provincial

32 Though national assemblies might lapse, regional Estates were summoned regularly, particularly in the more independent provinces. The Estates of Burgundy, shown here, survived as long as the old régime.

Estates. Generally speaking, the number of deputies of towns also increased.

Estates also existed, at the end of the fifteenth century, in other provinces and regions – Guienne, Touraine, Limousin, Orléanais, Maine, Anjou, Marche, etc. – and there were even Estates subordinate, mainly for taxation assessment, to the larger provincial Estates. For example, those of Vivarais, Velay, and Gévaudan were attached to the Estates of Languedoc, and those of Charolais, Auxonne, and Mâconnais to the Estates of Burgundy. Many of the lesser Estates were to disappear in the sixteenth and seventeenth centuries; but some of the big ones, such as Languedoc and Brittany, were to last as long as the old régime.

They had come to form an essential part of it for taxation purposes and
had built up an efficient organization. In the intervals between sessions
the work of the Estates was carried on by officers whom they employed
(whether *greffier*, *trésorier*, or *syndics*) and by a committee charged to
carry out their decisions, to watch over the rights of the Estates, and
prepare for the following session. In France it was not the Estates-
General that mattered as part of the normal machinery of government
and as representative of the interests of powerful social groups; it was
the provincial Estates that counted. This was only natural in the
country which, until 1789, was the largest effectively organized
realm in Latin Christendom; the price to be paid for a formal political
unity was a respect for local rights and customs, and a centralized
parliament was probably a political impossibility before the eighteenth
century.

Nevertheless, the development of France was one of growing strength for the monarchy. In Germany the power of the monarchy, weakened by the Investiture Contest, was finally broken after the death of Frederick II in 1250. Authority passed increasingly into the hands of the princes; but Germans could not forget that they were part of the empire, still bound by some ties to the emperor. From this situation arose complications for the representative institutions of Germany, for some clergy, nobles, and towns continued to owe immediate loyalty to the emperor, whereas others were directly subject to a lesser prince, and only indirectly to the emperor. Most of the comital families and greater landowners (*Freie Herren*) originally belonged to the empire, and had a certain independence in relation to the princes. Earlier there was a great gulf between them and the vassals of the princes and the Church, and the *ministeriales*, who had often risen from serfdom in the service of a prince or prelate. In the later thirteenth century this latter group was fusing to form the *Ritterschaft*; and in some states it remained distinct from the *Herren*. Such was the case in Austria, where the *Herren* and *Ritterschaft* formed in consequence separate estates or *Stände* in the *Landtag*. But in most parts of Germany the *Herren* and *Ritterschaft* became sufficiently united in the fourteenth century into the nobility (*Adel*) to form one single estate (*Stand*). Even so, the distinction between great nobles and lesser was sufficiently distinct in some states, such as Saxony and Brandenburg, for the greater nobility to be summoned personally (*Schriftsassen*) and the lesser nobility (*Amtsassen*) to appear merely by proxy, by representatives elected for their local group.

It was long thought a mark of distinction to hold immediately from the emperor, so lesser nobles, whose social and economic status was precarious, often made a special point of refusing to participate in the *Landtag* of a prince. This typically lasted until the sixteenth century when the power of the imperial free knights (*Reichsritter*) was broken. The same was true of towns, a few of which, such as Hamburg and Frankfurt-am-Main, were sufficiently wealthy and powerful to retain their status as imperial free cities until the end of the empire in 1806; they could not be summoned to any mere provincial assembly (*Landtag*), but only to the *Reichstag*, the imperial Diet. The prelates had a stronger social status, and could therefore accept invitations to participate in *Landtage* without so much risk to their position; all the same, they were on the whole cautious until the later fourteenth century, when the Great Schism in the Church had begun. Then the conflicts between princes often induced them to attend the *Landtag* to defend the privileges of their order; if they did so, they commonly formed the first estate or sometimes joined the *Herren* to emphasize that as prelates they still held directly from the emperor. The greatest bishops and archbishops continued however to remain outside *Landtage* – at any rate until the Reformation had destroyed their power in Protestant areas.

By the later fourteenth century *Landtage* were common in the now fairly independent principalities of Germany, and the usual pattern was one of three estates – clergy, nobles, towns. The pattern varied, however, and so did the pace of evolution. For example, in certain regions deputies of towns were convoked as early as the end of the thirteenth century, whereas in areas of late urban development, such as Styria and Carinthia, the towns were not represented until the end of the fourteenth century. Generally speaking, the princes had a common motive for summoning towns, in that they needed the financial help of the towns for the work of government, especially for raising troops and making war. But the number of towns summoned, and their influence in the *Landtage*, varied very much. In the states of north-east Germany, such as Brandenburg, the influence of the lords was by the fifteenth century becoming so great that many towns were mediatized – that is, made subject, not directly to the emperor or even the prince of the empire, but mediately to the local lord, lay or clerical – and therefore had no part in the *Landtag*. Those which were represented saw their influence shrinking as the power of the lords became ever more dominant. In the assemblies of south-western Germany, however, the towns were often numerous and important. In Württemberg, for example, the *Landtag* in 1498 comprised thirteen prelates, thirty knights, and one hundred and twenty urban deputies from forty towns. Moreover, the towns often had such administrative influence over the surrounding countryside that they could claim to speak on behalf of the surrounding region. In a principality like Brandenburg, on the other hand, it was the nobility which could and did increasingly speak on behalf of the countryside and its peasantry.

It was rare for the peasantry to be directly represented in a *Landtag*; and, as might be expected, it was most likely to happen in those areas where the peasantry enjoyed an unusual degree of economic and social independence. In East Friesland, for example, there was a prosperous peasant freeholder class which, rearing cattle in the marshes, was difficult to control. Hence the peasants formed the third order in the *Landtag*, after the knights and towns. In the Tyrol the hardy peasants of the mountain valleys were, like the Swiss, so inaccessible to knightly power that they had to be given a large degree of administrative and judicial autonomy; and here, from the fourteenth century, the peasants regularly formed the fourth group in the *Landtag*.

The history of the German *Landtage* was not one of continuous rise to the sixteenth century and then uninterrupted decline. The breakdown of the authority of the emperor during the Great Interregnum after the death of Frederick II in 1250 was a time of great confusion. Except for the border lands in the north-east and south-east, there were scarcely any well-defined states, only collections of fiefs, allodial lands, bits of counties, areas of varied and overlapping jurisdiction. Hence the estates that were forming did not yet have the sense of belonging to a state; and the princes thought of their lands as patrimonies to be divided among their children, not as states with a unity to be preserved and defended. So it was a time of confusion in modes of consultation. Princes sometimes consulted estates, usually to try to get money from them, but not on any consistent plan. Often towns or knights, or towns and knights, joined together in unions (*Einungen*) to resist by force attempts of princes or great nobles to levy contributions which, in the absence of any clearly defined legal states, were apt to look like mere robberies. So successful was resistance on the whole that in the early fourteenth century princes commonly desisted from demanding money from the estates and managed as best they could.

But in 1356 the Emperor Charles IV issued the Golden Bull which removed the previous uncertainty as to who were imperial electors. The seven electors were given nearly sovereign rights in their lands; they could coin money and judge without appeal, and it was high treason to rebel against them. The lands of the lay electors were to descend by primogeniture, to prevent division of territories and confusion as to who were the electors. For the moment the princes who were not declared electors were hostile to the new arrangement, as were the towns; but the long-term effects of the Golden Bull were great. The rule of primogeniture encouraged a dynastic sense in the electorates, and this eventually proved infectious by example. The electors directly, and other princes by imitation, were encouraged to try to consolidate their power over the territories they ruled and to turn them from mere patrimonies into dynastic states. This encouraged resistance from revived leagues of towns; some of the biggest, like the Hanseatic, Swabian and Rhenish leagues, were too widespread and powerful to be subjugated to a particular principality, but some of the smaller ones operated within a state framework. Similarly the knights formed leagues, some of which operated across Germany, like the Horner, Falkner, and St Georg Bund leagues, while some were local and concerned to resist a particular ruler. A particularly defiant league was that of knights and townsmen at Lüneburg, formed in 1392; in 1396 the Duke of Brunswick-Lüneburg had to storm the town to defeat it.

The turbulence and strength of the unions often prompted the rulers to summon regular assemblies of estates, as a preferable alternative to threats and coercion from irregular unions. But regular convocations of estates did not necessarily bring relief if the position of the princes continued weak, as it did in the fourteenth century in many of the principalities. In Brandenburg, for example, the ruling family changed four times in one century; in Meissen the margraves were impoverished by the declining yield of the silver-mines and weakened by the division of the inheritance between heirs; in Bavaria repeated partitions were followed by strife between the heirs. This enabled the estates to insist on conditions and increase their power. Thus in 1356 a committee of noblemen and commoners was set up in Upper Bavaria to supervise a tax on cattle; two years later a similar committee was appointed in Lower Bavaria. In 1363 the Duke of Upper Bavaria had to promise to appoint a council from those resident in Upper Bavaria on the advice of the estates, and in 1393 he had to undertake not to start any war without their assent and to let them meet as often as they thought fit, to discuss the needs of the country and its rulers. When, in 1504, the Landshut line of the Wittelsbachs died out, the Estates of the divided territories proclaimed the unity of the duchy; and in 1505 the united *Landtag* insisted that the duke should confirm its privileges before it swore allegiance to him. Seven years earlier the *Landtag* of Württemberg had claimed to decide which wars were legitimate, and when Duke Eberhard fled the country, it declared him deposed and published a fundamental law.

33 Duke Eberhard of Württemberg with his noble councillors, *c.* 1400. This council was a forerunner of one of the more vigorous and effective of the *Landtage*, which deposed another Eberhard a century later.

Not all the lands of the empire had Estates so vigorous as this; those of Hesse and the Palatinate, for example, were able to exert their power only fitfully. But many other principalities, like Brandenburg, Saxony, Cleves, and Mark, had by the end of the fifteenth century well-established Estates, with considerable privileges, standing committees, and permanent officials. The princes were by this time often coming to a clearer realization of their role as rulers of states, not merely as heads of families; and, as Albert Achilles did in Brandenburg, they could use the Estates in the administration, especially in taxation. For the time being this dualism could exist; the history of the next two centuries would show whether it could continue as the power of the princes grew.

THE LOW COUNTRIES

It was not everywhere that the Estates favoured a wider unity; they tended on the contrary to resist unification if it did not appear to them to be founded on tradition. Thus in the Netherlands the dukes of Burgundy tried hard in the fifteenth century to achieve united assemblies for the whole of their lands, but in spite of repeated meetings of representatives of towns, it was not possible to get together a States-General until 1464. The various provinces insisted on keeping their own Estates with jealously guarded rights; until 1585 the States-General did not include the Estates of Luxembourg, which protested that they were separate, or of the provinces of Guelders, Friesland, Overijssel, Groningen, and Ommeland, acquired by Charles V between 1523 and 1536.

In any case, the creation of a States-General for the lands of the dukes of Burgundy did not mean the supersession of the Estates of the participating provinces. The latter were very suspicious of concessions that might be wrung or wheedled from the former; and the delegates to the States-General were given carefully defined powers. If any demands were made at the States-General for which they did not have a clear mandate, they had to refer back to their constituents. When, in January 1473, Charles the Bold summoned the States-General to Bruges to demand an aid of 600,000 crowns a year for ten years, the deputies had to go home to consult. In February they reassembled and agreed to an aid of 500,000 crowns, some for six years, some for three years. The Duke at once accepted the more favourable offer and sent back those deputies who had offered aid for only three years. When they returned, they accepted the term of six years. Though this was a cumbrous arrangement, the States-General could not be by-passed, for in 1477 Duchess Marie of Burgundy was forced to grant the Great Privilege, by which the States-General must be consulted on many important issues, including the levy of taxation and the declaration of any war; they were to be allowed to meet where and when they wished. Eleven years later Maximilian had to agree that they should assemble every year. Though he and later rulers tried to pretend that these concessions had been exacted by force and were therefore invalid, the governments of the Netherlands did in fact summon the States-General every year until the troubles of Philip II's reign; between 1464 and 1576 there were about 160 meetings of the States-General.

The provincial Estates which chose the deputies to the States-General were mostly composed of nobles, clergy and towns in the usual way. But the maritime provinces had risen to great wealth through industry and trade, Flanders in the twelfth century, Brabant, Holland, and Zeeland somewhat later. This gave them great importance, and within these provinces it was the towns which dominated

the scene. In Flanders the Estates assembly was composed (except for the recognition of a new prince) of the representatives of the three great cities of Bruges, Ghent and Ypres, and the urban-dominated Franc de Bruges, together with representative clergy; the nobles were absent. In the Estates of Holland the nobles had only one vote, whereas eighteen towns had a vote each. In Zeeland the nobles had one vote to six for the towns. In Brabant nobles had a larger place in the Estates, but the towns predominated; it was they which took the lead in obtaining in 1356 the great charter of privileges known later as the *Joyeuse Entrée*. The relative wealth of the provinces may be seen from the fact that, at the end of the fifteenth century, Flanders and Brabant each paid a quarter of the total levy, Holland one-sixth, and Zeeland one-quarter of Holland's share. So between them these four provinces paid nearly three-quarters of the whole taxation, and their

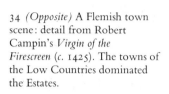

34 *(Opposite)* A Flemish town scene: detail from Robert Campin's *Virgin of the Firescreen* (c. 1425). The towns of the Low Countries dominated the Estates.

35 *(Right)* Maximilian, son of the Emperor Frederick III, was chosen by the States-General as a husband for Marie of Burgundy.

towns expected to exercise corresponding political power in the provincial Estates and the States-General.

These powers reflected the important political role of the Flemish towns at various decisive points in the history of the Netherlands. In 1477, for example, they virtually decided the choice of husband for the heiress of Burgundy, the Duchess Marie, after the death of her father Charles the Bold, and after her death in 1482 they dictated terms to her husband Maximilian as to both the custody of his son Philip and the conclusion of peace with Louis XI. These facts are useful reminders of the variety of different social structures on which parliaments were founded. There were towns in the states that developed on the eastern borders of Germany – Poland, Bohemia, and Hungary – but usually they had not sufficient economic vitality to withstand the other social forces at work. The more important

81

of them, as in Transylvania, often had a strong foreign element, usually German, which caused them to stand apart from the body politic in attempted independence. Generally speaking, however, their political importance was in decline, even before the end of the fifteenth century. The relatively few which maintained their economic vitality, like Danzig, strove to achieve a greater independence; the rest were increasingly dominated by the nobility. For diverse as the history of these lands is in detail, they have one important feature in common – namely that, unlike England or France, they did not have monarchies which succeeded in dominating the social structure and the constitutional forms. On the contrary, the control that the king could exercise became weaker as the generations went by. This was reflected in the development of the Estates in these countries.

RISE OF THE SLAV AND MAGYAR MAGNATES

In Poland the relatively flat plains and absence of formidable mountain ranges enabled military leaders, from the time of Boleslav the Mighty (992–1025) onwards, to unify large areas under their control. Though impressive in appearance, the large realm thus created had many of the defects which, earlier, led to the fall of the Carolingian Empire. The kings regarded their realm as a family estate and divided it among their sons. The administration could not, in the primitive circumstances, be centralized and bureaucratic; it depended largely on the selection by the kings of local magnates as officials or as knights, who were rewarded with land. But the old tribal divisions had never been erased, and the effect of royal policies and royal weakness was to give provincial loyalties a continued vitality and new leaders, armed with a certain royal authority and prestige. This was reflected in the twelfth and thirteenth centuries in the enhanced power of the greater nobility, on the one hand in increased powers of administration and justice over the populations of their domains, and on the other hand in the development of provincial assemblies of lay nobles and great ecclesiastics who tended to dominate the conduct of affairs in their province.

So marked was this development that it threatened the disintegration of the country, which became divided among various scions of the Piast dynasty. The bishops of Breslau and Cammin, for example, created principalities for themselves, and the *voivodes* of Cracow added to their title the formula *Dei gratia*. The Germanized towns of western Poland asserted their independence; the peasantry, prospering from demands for Polish cereals in western Europe, were restive; the clergy remembered the claims of the Church and demanded further privileges. The magnates, feeling their social position threatened, turned to the lesser nobility and gentry for support. The solidarity of the nobles forged in this way bore fruit at the beginning of the four-teenth century. Legal privileges and exemption from taxation were extended to all noble proprietors. During the fourteenth century the Polish nobility began to think of itself as one estate, the *communitas nobilium*, with common privileges and common aims.

The reunification of Poland in 1320 under Vladislav I did not arrest this trend. It was his greater son, Casimir the Great, who confirmed the privileges of the nobility or *szlachta*; and when he died without male heirs in 1370, his son-in-law, Ludwig the Great of Hungary, could only secure recognition by making the momentous Pact of Koszyce with the nobility. In return for the entail of the crown on one of his daughters, he declared the *szlachta* free of taxation in per-petuity and promised that offices should be restricted to them. The pact created an evil precedent for fresh concessions from the monarchy at subsequent accessions. When Ludwig died, the nobility compelled his heiress Hedwig to marry Jagiello, Grand Duke of Lithuania, in order to secure the union of the two states; and he, recognizing the social forces on which his power was based, began to summon meetings of a central Diet or *Sejm*. This was composed of nobility or officials of noble birth – bishops and high dignitaries of the state, *voivodes* and castellans – with representatives of cathedral chapters (also noble) and towns. Only the delegates of towns stood apart in status. In addition, the provincial Diets of Little and Great Poland were still summoned, as well as dietines or little Diets, for *voivodies* and 'Lands'; all these Diets were composed of nobles.

During the reigns of Jagiello (or Vladislav II) and his son, the *Sejm* was summoned at least every year and sometimes twice a year. From the accession of Vladislav Jagiello each king had to be elected by the *Sejm*, which took the opportunity to limit his powers further. Gradually the power even to make concessions was taken away from him. In 1454 the king had to undertake that no new taxes or levies of the army should be made without the consent of the dietines, com-posed of the nobility. Thenceforward the *Sejm* decreed the concessions. To maintain any independence the king had to try to play off the dietines against the *Sejm*. This was increasingly difficult to do, for during the fifteenth century the *Sejm* included not only the bishops, great dignitaries, *voivodes*, and castellans, who came to form the Senate, presided over by the king, but also, by 1493, representatives of the dietines, who came to form a Chamber of Deputies. A few representatives of towns were summoned to this chamber, but their number was soon limited to representatives of the capital and a few other towns and they were deprived of voting powers. In 1496 the *Sejm* forbade townsmen to acquire lands, thus ensuring that outside the towns the proprietors were all noble; and in 1505 was promulgated the famous constitution *Nihil Novi*, which instituted a sort of condominium between king, Senate, and Chamber of Deputies. The nobility had triumphed in the state, and the *Sejm* and the dietines, whether provincial or local, were the most important instruments of the nobility.

The nobles of Hungary never managed to win so complete a victory as those of Poland, nor were the privileges and constitution of the Hungarian Diet so well defined as those of the Polish *Sejm*. But the constitutional developments in the two countries followed similar lines. The successors of King Stephen (997–1038) relied on local officials who quickly became a new aristocracy, merging with the previous landowners to form a magnate class. When, in the early thirteenth century, King Andrew II tried to rule arbitrarily and autocratically, the real balance of social forces was revealed in the Golden Bull that he was forced to concede in 1222. Though it speaks of the protection of the poor, most of the clauses were concerned with aristocratic privileges. The nobles were to be protected against imprisonment without judicial examination and sentence, they were exonerated from taxes, the king could visit their villages only by invitation, and he could not make war without their consent, nor compel them to serve in the army save when an enemy invaded the land.

Before the monarchy had time to recover its power, the terrible Tartar invasion intervened in 1241. King Bela fled and the land fell a prey to the Tartar fury. Though Bela was able to return when the Tartars retired to Mongolia on the death of Genghis Khan's heir, his dynasty was fatally weakened, and rivals from Bohemia, Austria, and France plotted to seize the opportunity of conquest. When the last Arpad, Andrew III, died in 1301, a bloody war of succession raged for eight years; and when eventually the House of Anjou triumphed in the person of Charles Robert, the magnates had taken advantage of the struggle for the crown to increase their power greatly. By skilful administration and an imperialist policy Charles Robert and his son Ludwig the Great restored the prestige of the monarchy, which by the time of Ludwig's death had secured for the Hungarian Crown a vast territory extending from the Baltic to the Adriatic, as well as the kingdom of Naples. But in 1370 he died without a male heir, and another tussle for the throne began. A certain revival of the power of the Crown took place under the Emperor Sigismund, but when he died in 1437 leaving only a daughter, a twenty-year struggle for the succession took place.

It was in these years of strife, from 1437 to 1457, that the Hungarian Diet grew into a permanent institution. Already at the end of the fourteenth century the growing Turkish peril had meant that the monarchy needed increased financial and military support, and in 1389 four nobles were summoned from each county assembly to the Diet. The county assembly was, like the Polish dietine, a meeting of all the nobles of the area; and from the middle of the fifteenth century it came to be accepted that the national Diet should include not only the prelates and great magnates, but representatives of the lesser nobles and the gentry. Thenceforward the nobility came to be conceived of as the political nation. Deputies of the towns did attend regularly from 1441, but they had to be content to watch and report on the proceedings of the Diet without being allowed to take any effective part in them. In this period from 1437 to 1457 it came to be accepted that the consent of the Diet was necessary to legislation and the levy of taxes.

The next sixty years after 1457 saw the final victory of the nobility in the Diet and in the Hungarian state. The popular and able noble-man Matthew Hunyadi (Matthias Corvinus), who made himself king in 1457, was strong and skilful enough to insist on regular elections of gentry representatives of the counties and to keep some control of the proceedings of the Diet. But when he was followed in 1490 by the weak descendant of the Jagellon dynasty, Vladislav II, the gentry were able to assert themselves in tumultuous fashion, and edicts of 1492 and 1498 actually ordered the entire gentry to attend the Diet. The meetings of the Diet became riotous assemblies, with exaggerated demands by the nobility and gentry not only on the king but against the peasantry.

85

36 King Matthias Corvinus of Hungary (1458–90).

But though the Turkish threat was coming ever nearer, the nobility and gentry did nothing to organize resistance to it. In desperation the chancellor, Bakács, Archbishop of Esztergom, obtained a papal bull proclaiming a crusade against the Turks. The bull was read in April 1514 from the church of Buda Castle. Immediately thousands of peasants responded to the call and were armed for the Peasants' Crusade. Their leader Dósza diverted the army of scores of thousands of armed peasants to social revolution, and a ferocious social war began. The alarmed nobility defeated the rebels with great difficulty, and only after unspeakable atrocities on both sides. The defeat of the peasants had social and constitutional consequences momentous for Hungary's future. Socially the peasants were reduced to bondsmen of the landowners; constitutionally Stephen Werboczy, an authority on public law, presented to the Diet a *Corpus Juris*, or fundamental law. Henceforth the Hungarian state was to be a partnership between king and nation; and the nation was conceived to be the nobility and higher clergy, who spoke for the rest. The king received the power to exercise political rule from the nation which elected him, and he had to recognize this by oath before he was crowned with the crown of St Stephen.

After the disaster of Mohács in 1526, when King Ludwig fell before the victorious Turks and the crown passed to Ferdinand of Habsburg, the Austrian government tried to whittle down the implications of the edict of the *Corpus Juris* or *Tripartitum*. In 1530 it insisted that the custom of personal attendance of the gentry in the Diet should end; and it would not brook the interference of the Diet in diplomacy and the financing of the army, as had frequently occurred under the weak Jagellons. Nevertheless the concept that the nobility was the political nation was to last until 1848, and was to influence the role of the Diet in all its vicissitudes.

The history of Bohemia differs much from that of Hungary, but there are considerable elements of similarity in the development of their Estates. The extinction of the House of Premysl in Bohemia in 1306 led to a struggle for the succession, as had happened in Hungary when the House of Arpad ended there in 1301. And as Hungary had its Ludwig the Great (1342–82), so in the same period Bohemia was ruled by its greatest king, the Holy Roman Emperor Charles IV (1346–78). His concern for the unity of his Bohemian realm was shown by his holding of general Diets from all provinces, even though they opposed his attempt to codify and revise the law in his *Majestas Carolina* because of their attachment to more primitive custom.

This period of strong monarchy was followed, as in Hungary, by several generations in which the Crown was weakened and disputed; indeed in Bohemia the Hussite wars that began with the accession of the Emperor Sigismund in 1419 inaugurated a time when the power of the Crown was virtually in abeyance. The confiscations of Church property by the aristocracy and the almost incessant civil war caused a rapid decline in the economic and political position of the peasantry and towns that was in the end to be fatal to the efficiency of the Hussite armies. Constitutionally it meant that the Diet or *Sněm* came swiftly to be dominated by the nobles, for the knights and burgesses found the expense of attendance intolerable, the proceedings frustrating and tumultuous. The meetings were brief, irregular, and ill organized. The *Sněm* was unable to provide good government; but by 1440 the desire for this was so general, especially among the lower orders, who suffered cruelly from the continuous violence and rapine, that the Diet of 1440 decreed the division of the realm into districts, significantly called *landfridy*, 'peace districts', each with a head or *hejtman* and a local council of lords, knights, and sometimes burgesses, with very extensive powers of enforcing order and exercising justice. The resemblance of the Bohemian *landfridy* to the Hungarian county courts and the Polish *sejmiki* (local assemblies) is striking, all the more so as the *landfridy* in the sixteenth century came to be increasingly dominated by the nobility.

MINERS, PEASANTS, AND BURGHERS

The nobility did not triumph so completely everywhere in the outer lands of western Christendom. In Scandinavia the peasant farmers and artisans remained free, at any rate until the sixteenth century, to a degree unusual in western Europe, and this relatively high economic and political status was reflected in the organization of the Diets. In Denmark, it is true, the power of the nobility increased in the thirteenth and fourteenth centuries against both the peasantry and the king. For example, in 1282 the nobility forced King Erik Klipping to concede a Great Charter in which he had to promise, among other things, that he would summon a *Danehof*, or assembly of nobles, every year, and govern with its advice and aid. This concession did not save Erik from murder in 1286, nor his successors from repeated depositions and almost continuous browbeating by the aristocracy. By 1468 the monarchy had been so weakened that King Christian I called representatives of the burghers and of the free peasants, as some counterpoise to the nobility, to what was probably the first regular meeting of the Diet (held in Kalundborg) that replaced the *Danehof*. Henceforth for over a hundred years the *Stændermøde* or *Rigsdag* was composed of four estates – nobles, clergy, townsmen, and peasants. The *Rigsdag* claimed extensive powers; without it the king could not declare wars, fix taxes, or nominate officials. But by the end of the sixteenth century the peasants had mostly sunk into serfdom; their representatives were soon to disappear from the *Rigsdag*, and the deputies of the clergy and of the towns found it hard to withstand the overbearing influence of the nobility.

In Sweden, much more mountainous and forested and more sparsely populated, the peasants and artisans were economically more independent of the nobility, and better able to hold their own against them. In 1435 there was a formidable revolt against Erik of Pomerania, the king of the united Scandinavian kingdoms. The revolt was led by Engelbrekt Engelbrektsson, a man of gentle birth but also a mineowner who had many sympathetic links with the miners and, through

37 Gustavus Vasa, elected King of Sweden in 1523 by a *Riksdag* which included representatives of burghers and peasants.

them, with the free peasantry. King Erik had formidable resources, many of the Swedish nobles disapproved of the rising, and Engelbrekt had to get support where he could. And so he turned to the powerful miners of Dalarna and their allies, the peasants and the burghers. He therefore called together at Arboga a great assembly which included not only nobles and clergy but representatives of towns, miners, and peasants. It met to receive, not – as parliaments so often did – demands for money but a stirring appeal for support against the Danes; it responded by electing Engelbrekt regent. But Engelbrekt had aroused the fatal jealousy of some of the nobles, who murdered him in the next year (1436). Nevertheless he had begun a tradition which was not forgotten, of appealing to the miners and peasants to support the cause of national independence.

When in 1471 the Danes were defeated by the Swedes at the battle of Brunkeberg, the new young regent of Sweden, Sten Sture, made much use of the support of burghers and peasants, in numerous meetings of the *Riksdag* to which they were regularly summoned. His kinsman and political heir, Gustavus Vasa, continued this policy. After Sture's death, Christian II of Denmark made great efforts to re-establish the union of Denmark and Sweden; but after his Blood Bath of Stockholm in 1520 provoked the Swedes into revolt, Gustavus Vasa sealed his success in 1523 by holding a *Riksdag* at Strängnäs, in which, along with members of the nobility and clergy, were representatives of towns, mines and peasantry. This assembly elected him king; and an assembly with the same elements meeting four years later, at Västerås, at his instigation introduced the Lutheran Reformation officially into Sweden. The burghers and peasants thus participated in this decade in decisions of the first importance. This was not merely at the instance of the nobility, for it was the peasants at Västerås who took the lead in urging Gustavus to return when he talked in despair of abdication.

Not all peripheral countries with weak monarchies and comparatively primitive economic and social structures made provision for peasant representation. In Scotland the kings of the fourteenth and fifteenth centuries tried intermittently to imitate their more powerful neighbours, the kings of England, in the organization of a parliament; but though they managed by perseverance to get the burgesses to attend with regularity by the late fifteenth century, the gentry succeeded a century earlier in evading attendance. The kings were too

38 The arms of the Swiss canton of Uri, painted on glass *c.* 1500, express the pride of a warrior peasantry that has become a ruling class.

weak to make them come, and by this time it was ceasing to be worth the effort; for from 1367 the estates chose certain persons 'to hold the parliament', while the rest obtained leave to go home to attend to their own affairs. By the early sixteenth century the only functions left to the estates were to choose the Lords of the Articles at the opening of a parliament and to give a perfunctory approval to their acts at the end of the parliament. Compared with the English Parliament, the medieval Scottish parliament was insignificant; and it was dominated by the nobility.

On the other hand, a state that was slowly forming in the heart of western Europe was controlled by peasants and townsmen. The Swiss Confederation, which had begun with the pact of 1291 between the three forest cantons of Uri, Schwyz, and Unterwald, had by the sixteenth century expanded into a network of extraordinary complexity. Some of the full members were rural cantons, some were town cantons. Some new arrivals were allowed, like Basle, Schaffhausen, and Appenzell, to become full members; others remained allies, like Haut Valais, the Leagues of Grisons, Neuchâtel, St Gall, Geneva. Some people were mere subjects of the cantons. The constitutions of the towns had a great variety, though most of them had in the early days a general assembly of burgesses (which was fairly big and open to new entrants) and an elected head or *Schultheiss*. The tendency was for the *Schultheiss* to be increasingly helped by a Grand Council and a Little Council that shrank in numbers, and for the coveted rank of burgess to become increasingly difficult to attain. Some towns, like Basle, Zürich, and Schaffhausen, came to be dominated by wealthy and oligarchic gilds. The rural cantons remained more open in government, with general assemblies of peasant citizens (*Landsgemeinde*) and a representative head (*Landammann*). The Leagues of the Grisons – the leagues of God's House, Grisons, and Ten Jurisdictions – formed a loose union and set up a Diet to discuss common concerns; but this Diet or *Bundestag* was subject to frequent referenda, and had little real power. Similarly the *Bundestag* of the whole federation reflected the anxiety of the member cantons not to lose their sovereignty. All decisions had to be unanimous, and the delegates had the strictest mandates from their cantons. It is not surprising that united action was virtually impossible; military campaigns, like the conquest of the Vaud, were usually undertaken by one or two cantons.

In Italy there was an equally bewildering variety of constitutions, with representative assemblies in evidence in only a few states. In northern Italy the cities established their independence of the empire in the twelfth and thirteenth centuries; and though they developed varied constitutions which passed through fascinating changes, they were, generally speaking, not extensive enough to need representative assemblies of the type of a parliament or assembly of estates. In some of the bigger states representative assemblies appeared for a while, but only in Naples, Sicily, and Sardinia were they of any lasting importance. In the States of the Church only the parliament of the March of Ancona had any significance; and even here the papal nuncios made it very clear that the only purpose of the parliament was to make itself useful to papal administration. In Montferrat a parliament developed in the fourteenth century, but by the fifteenth century the rulers developed a policy of centralization and the competence of the parliament was limited to deliberating the amount of the subsidy. The last sign of life was in 1502 when it refused to sanction the billeting of French soldiers – who were billeted all the same. In Piedmont a much more impressive parliament developed in the fourteenth century, with powers to vote taxes, initiate laws, and influence government policy. But when the French overran Piedmont in 1536, they used the estates to help their administration, so when Duke Emanuel Philibert recovered power in 1559 he regarded the parliament as having forfeited its powers and rights by its treason. After 1560 he never summoned it again. In Friuli, too, a powerful parliament developed in the fourteenth century, and the council of parliament was greatly used by the patriarch in his administration – military, financial, and administrative. But in 1420 the patriarchate was conquered by Venice and the powers of the parliament were drastically reduced.

By the early sixteenth century the Italian parliaments which had most importance were all in Spanish dominions. This was no accident; the Spanish kings were used to *Cortes* in the Iberian peninsula and regarded their collaboration on taxation and the investigation of grievances as a natural part of the government machinery. Indeed, so obvious did this seem that Ferdinand the Catholic actually increased the role of both the Sardinian and the Neapolitan parliaments – something that needs to be remembered in view of the common assumption that the policy of the Catholic kings was to make their government more centralized and autocratic. In Sardinia the first general assembly – hardly a proper parliament – was summoned by Peter IV of Aragon in 1355 in order to secure his authority against the Genoese; and the next important meeting, held in 1421, was also designed to reconcile rebels against the Crown of Aragon. But it was not until Ferdinand the Catholic summoned in 1481 a parliament, which lasted until 1485, primarily to secure taxes to protect the island from the Turkish menace, that the powers of the parliament became important and well established. By the end of his reign it was generally accepted that it was the role of parliament to grant taxes and to advise on legislative and administrative matters, even to the point of asserting its authority against the viceroys on occasion.

In Naples the Angevin kings occasionally summoned large meetings from the late thirteenth century onwards, but these were extraordinary political assemblies of irregular composition and purpose rather than a regular parliamentary institution. It was only after the conquest of the kingdom by Alfonso of Aragon in 1442 that a true parliament was organized. A 'general parliament' meeting in 1443 at Benevento was limited to the nobility, yet it was the first great national assembly. Meetings were fitful, however, until the conquest of the realm by Ferdinand of Spain. He and the governors he appointed seem to have thought that each possession of the Crown ought to have its own *Cortes* to vote taxes and present grievances and requests, so a much better organized parliament was formed in Naples consisting of nobles, prelates, and townsmen. This parliament met about forty times in the sixteenth century. It had to be convoked about every two years, when the main tax or *donativo* expired; so firm had the rule become that the parliament must approve of the grant of taxation. And the embassies of the parliament to Madrid could be so formidable that the viceroys did their best to prevent them.

It was, however, the parliament of Sicily which displayed the most vitality of them all. It began to be organized as early as 1296 by the Aragonese Frederick II. During the fourteenth century the life of the island was too troubled for the parliament to be anything but irregular and ineffective in its meetings, but when King Martin I of Aragon had conquered the island after 1395, he was strong enough to reorganize the government. After his assembly at Syracuse in 1398, the parliament of Sicily began to assume the functions and structure of the *Cortes* of Aragon and Catalonia, as was evident in its internal organization, a close similarity of procedure, and the creation of a permanent Deputation which supervised the levy and the spending of the *donativo* or financial aid. In a short time it became strong enough to intervene in questions of succession to the throne. In 1410 a parliamentary committee decided between three claimants, and in 1460 the parliament gave valuable help to Ferdinand the Catholic against the claims of his half-brother, Charles of Viana. In gratitude Ferdinand abolished all taxes on the island, except for the ordinary *collette* or customary taxes; but financial necessity forced him later to go back on this concession. Indeed, the powers claimed by the Sicilian *Parlamento* were so great that he found himself driven to oppose them somewhat, instead of encouraging them as in Sardinia and Naples. In the middle of the fifteenth century the parliament had forced King Alfonso V to agree that taxes were granted only in return for the acceptance of parliamentary petitions for confirmation of privileges or redress of grievances; he had also had to agree that laws were not merely the expression of the royal will but contracts between king and parliament. Ferdinand would not consent to these contractual notions. Even so, the Sicilian parliament remained in his reign a powerful organization, well organized in three *bracci* or estates of prelates, nobles, and towns, very conscious of its own dignity and importance, and eager to defend the laws and privileges of Sicily and of its members. And, on the whole, both king and viceroy were very ready to respect the parliament and to work with it.

This was an attitude characteristic of many other rulers of this period: to find their parliaments often tiresome and factious in detail, to realize that they needed constant surveillance and management, but to accept them as part of the traditions and the constitutions of their realms, and to make use of them in the work of government, especially in taxation. Even this brief survey will perhaps have sufficed to show how varied were these parliaments in composition, functions, and frequency of meeting. But it should also be clear that parliamentary institutions, though not universal, were very general in western Christendom, and were in 1500 regarded as normal parts of the machinery of government. By 1700 the position had changed; and one of the main purposes of the next chapter will be to show how and why, by that date, assemblies of estates had come to be regarded as exceptional, and usually anachronistic in organization and outlook.

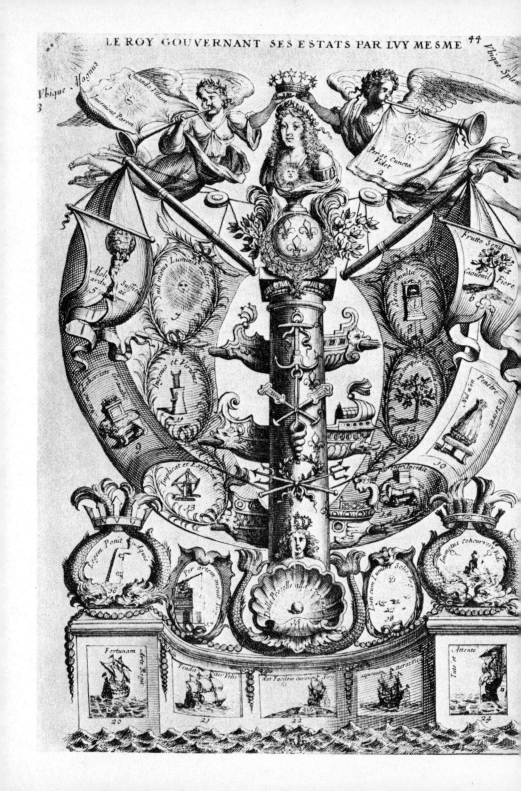

IV PARLIAMENTS AND AUTOCRATS:
THE END OF AN ERA

THE DECLINE OF THE SPANISH CORTES

At the beginning of the sixteenth century, even the most acute observer would have been hard put to it to say what was the general trend in the fortunes of parliaments. Against the decline in the fortunes of parliaments in Spain and Italy, he would have had to set an increase of power in most countries of northern Europe, especially in Poland and in the United Netherlands. It was only during the sixteenth century that not only the rulers but enlightened thinkers generally saw the best hopes for strong and efficient government, catering for the prosperity and internal peace of the realm, in an autocratic régime. It then came to seem obvious that if parliaments could be put to sleep, this would be a wise course for the prince to adopt; and if parliaments were too strongly embedded in tradition to be ignored, they must be rendered innocuous and indeed harnessed to the efficiency of auto-cratic government.

It was in Spain, where the *Cortes* had been so powerful in the four-teenth and fifteenth centuries, that the most striking reversal of fortune occurred. The decline came first in the *Cortes* of Castile, where there were, as was pointed out in the last chapter, some serious weaknesses which strong monarchs could exploit. Already under the Catholic kings the *Cortes* had lost the initiative in legislation to the royal council. Under Philip the Handsome (1504–06) appeared a tendency to change the estate of towns into a closed corporation; the urban deputies claimed to belong to the class of knights, and insisted that representation should be limited to those towns that had traditionally enjoyed it.

The arrival of the Flemish-speaking Charles V, with his Flemish advisers, in 1517 led to a head-on clash with the towns in the *Cortes* of 1518. The court wished the towns to give their delegates full powers to grant another *servicio* or aid to enable Charles to undertake the expense of the imperial crown. The towns tried to bind their representatives by definite instructions, and in spite of pressure only

39 'The King, alone, ruling over his estates' – an allegorical engraving of Louis XIV, the epitome of royal absolutism.

eight out of eighteen towns voted for the tax. As soon as the King had gone to Germany, revolutión broke out. Soon radical elements gained control in the towns, and the old hostility between nobles and cities burst into flame. In April 1521 the Castilian nobles defeated the townsmen at the battle of Villalar. Thenceforward the towns had lost their power to resist the monarchy. The emperor was willing to respect their old right to vote taxes – as long as they voted them – but their petitions could be granted or refused as he chose. He was, however, short of money for all his expensive wars, and at the *Cortes* of Toledo in 1538 Charles proposed an excise tax on foodstuffs from which no one would be exempt. The nobles and clergy protested vigorously, and to avoid trouble from them, Charles gave way. Thenceforward the nobles were exempt from taxation and were never summoned to the *Cortes* again. By the end of the reign the Castilian *Cortes* had shrunk to the anomalous position of 'an assembly of the king's council with the deputies of the towns'.

The consequences of the decision of 1538 were far-reaching for the future of the Castilian *Cortes*. The nobility, taken into partnership by the Crown for the government of the Spanish empire at the cost of exemption from taxation, lost interest in the fate of the *Cortes*. The *hidalgos* (nobles) who represented the towns in the *Cortes* were themselves exempt from taxation as nobles, so they willingly voted taxes which would fall on the non-privileged classes, and the one remaining weapon of the *Cortes* for the defence of its privileges was allowed to rust. Philip II summoned the *Cortes* less than his father had done. By 1660 the deputies of the towns were so unimportant that they were thenceforward to be chosen by lot. By the time of the accession of Charles II in 1665 the *Cortes* had become so insignificant that it was not summoned, as it had always hitherto been, to receive the oath of the new king. In the same year his mother, the Regent Queen Maria Anna, issued a decree ordering the towns to agree their contributions without bothering to come to an assembly of the *Cortes*. For the rest of the century the *Cortes* of Castile did not meet.

The *Cortes* of Aragon had enjoyed greater privileges and developed a more effective machinery. It could not be divided or overridden by the methods employed in Castile. And Charles V did not use the opportunity of the crushing victory of Villalar to destroy the privileges of the *Cortes* of Aragon, for both Aragon and Catalonia were too poor and too turbulent to justify the provocation of an unnecessary crisis. Mountainous Aragon had always been a poor land; the commercial prosperity of Catalonia had declined with the expansion of Turkish power in the Mediterranean, and in the highlands of Catalonia brigandage was endemic. So Charles was content to make the oppressed but, for the present, lucrative peasantry of Castile the financial basis of his power in Spain, and to respect the prickly devotion of the Aragonese to their privileges. Seven-eighths of the population of Spain lived in Castile; the king resided there and governed Aragon by viceroys and councils. His demands on the *Cortes* of Aragon were modest, he respected their traditions, he summoned them infrequently, and they gave him no trouble.

In the following reign Philip II saw no reason to change the relationship of the king to his eastern kingdom until the crisis of 1592; but as the *Cortes* could help him little, he summoned only two sessions during the first twenty-six years of his reign. Then in 1592 his hunted secretary, Antonio Pérez, fled to Aragon and claimed the protection of the *justicia*, the powerful judicial official of the *Cortes* of Aragon. Philip struck at Pérez through his instrument, the Inquisition, which arrested Pérez on a charge of heresy; in consequence a rising in defence of the liberties of Aragon took place. The rising was supported by the lesser nobility and gentry; the peasants did not move, for they had nothing to gain from resisting the king or defending their fundamental privileges, the *fueros*. The rebels failed in their attempt to draw Catalonia and Valencia to their cause, and the absence of any political solidarity between Aragon, Catalonia and Valencia was laid bare. The revolt was crushed with an army brought from the Low Countries, and many officials of the Aragonese *Cortes*, from the *justicia* downwards, were executed. Philip was too much of a traditionalist to destroy the *Cortes* of Aragon; but he broke its capacity to resist the Crown. He asserted his right to appoint a non-Aragonese viceroy; the *Diputación del Reyno*, the permanent committee of the *Cortes*, was deprived of most of its control over the revenues and the regional guard of Aragon; the *justicia* became removable at the king's pleasure; and the Inquisition was sited permanently in the fortified palace of the Aljafería, to strike down the king's enemies as required.

Nevertheless the proud traditions of Aragon were still sufficiently strong to encourage its *Cortes* to defend its privileges if the monarchy was seen to be in difficulties; and as the *Cortes* of Catalonia and Valencia had not been concerned in the revolt of 1592, their privileges remained intact. In 1626 the Spanish monarchy was deeply involved in the ruinous expense of the Thirty Years War, at a time when Castile was plainly approaching exhaustion and the trade with the Spanish colonies was already showing signs of collapse. The minister of Philip IV, Olivares, was convinced that the answer was to press for fiscal uniformity, and in this cause from 1626 onwards he put increasing pressure on the *Cortes* of Aragon, Catalonia and Valencia to grant what he considered more adequate sums for the support of the Spanish armies. They appealed to their privileges; Olivares pressed more strongly as the tide of war turned against Spain. At last, in exasperation and misery, the Catalans revolted in 1640 and placed themselves under French protection. The Spanish monarchy was now so weak that it could recover Catalonia in 1652 only by reaffirming in 1653 all the Catalan privileges; the traditions of separatism had been revived and remained.

During the War of the Spanish Succession the English, Dutch and Austrian allies tried to find a foothold in Spain for their candidate, the Archduke Charles of Austria. In 1705 a British fleet attacked Barcelona and Lord Peterborough captured it in the name of the Archduke. The Catalans rose in his favour and the revolt spread to Aragon and Valencia. But in 1711 the Archduke became the Emperor Charles VI on the death of his brother, and the allies withdrew their support. As before, the provinces of Aragon, Catalonia and Valencia were insufficiently united to hold out against Castile. In 1714 Barcelona fell and the principality of Catalonia was overrun by Castilian armies. Philip V was now in a position to disregard the *fueros*, and so treat the inhabitants of the three provinces as conquered rebels. Aragon and Valencia had already been vanquished and were given a new form of government in 1707. The viceroys were replaced by governors, and the provinces of the Crown of Aragon were henceforth to be made to pay their full share of taxation. The *Cortes* of the eastern kingdom was incorporated into that of Castile.

Henceforward the Spanish monarchy legislated by decree, and the *Cortes* was reduced to an assembly of subservient flatterers. Characteristic was its protestation in 1760: 'O sire, the realm is prepared not only to swear an oath of fidelity and do rightful homage, but to perform whatever your Majesty may propose.' Thus low had sunk an institution whose predecessors, at any rate in the kingdom of Aragon, had in their time been the most remarkable representative assemblies

40 *(Left)* Ferdinand and Isabella adoring the Virgin and Child: painting by an unknown Spanish artist. Kneeling behind Ferdinand is Torquemada, General of the Inquisition. 41 *(Right)* Councillors of Barcelona listening to a sermon from Bishop Severo in 1681. Among the less important of their privileges was the right to remain covered in church.

in Europe. The proud *Cortes* of the Crown of Aragon had fallen for several reasons. From the time of the union of the Crowns the monarchy was not dependent on their co-operation; they did not support each other; in time of crisis much of the population felt that the *Cortes* represented only the interests of privileged groups; and the monarchy could bring in troops from outside Aragon to crush resistance there.

THE ESTATES OF FRANCE

In France the Estates-General suffered a still more complete eclipse. The behaviour of the assembly at Tours in 1484 – factious, demanding and mean – had discouraged the monarchy from summoning the Estates-General again for over seventy years. But then in 1560 the government fell into the hands of a woman, Catherine de Médicis, anxiously ruling on behalf of her infant son, and fearful of the tumults caused by the progress of the Huguenots. She hoped that the Estates-General would give her support against her opponents. But the Estates-General that met in 1560 at Orléans, though fertile in complaints and petitions, was barren when it came to producing the

101

desired subsidies, on the ground that the deputies did not have sufficient powers from their constituents; and the small Estates committee
of thirty-nine, which met next year at Pontoise, did no better for the
monarchy.

The experience was not encouraging to the Crown, but in 1576
the religious strife had become so serious that the new king, Henry III,
tried again. In France's situation of near-anarchy, there was sudden
enthusiasm for the Estates-General. One book, Hotman's *Franco-
Gallia* (1573), traced its origins back to Charlemagne, and declared
that its authority was permanent and sacrosanct. When the Estates
met at Blois, they proposed that the king should hand over all power
to a small committee of their body; but they refused to vote the supplies
so desperately needed by the government. In spite of this disappoint-
ment Henry felt constrained to summon the Estates again in 1588,
when he was at the mercy of the Catholic League and looked for a way
of escape. But he soon turned to another, more desperate, device, the
murder of the leaders of the Catholic League, and the Estates-General
scattered in confusion. A further blow was struck at its reputation as
an instrument of government in 1593, when the Duke of Mayenne,
head of the Catholic League, summoned an assembly from those
provinces of the north and centre of France that supported the
Catholic cause, to regulate the succession to the throne to the exclusion
of Henry of Navarre.

Henry's subsequent triumph made the actions of Mayenne and the
Estates seem not only inept but treasonable. In the fourteenth and
fifteenth centuries it had still been possible to think that the Estates-
General might be useful as an instrument of regular government; the
experiences of the wars of religion made it appear as a futile expedient
of times of crisis, an assembly productive only of expense, time-
wasting, impossible demands and factious discontent. In 1614 the
Queen-Mother, Marie de Médicis, confronted with a dangerous
aristocratic rebellion, had to buy time by summoning a meeting of
the Estates-General. Its indifference to the government's financial
difficulties, and the quarrels between the estates, seemed to confirm
all the criticisms of her dead husband, Henry IV. Early in 1615 the
Estates-General was dismissed, never to meet again until 1789. Until
the generation before the Revolution both supporters and critics of
the government were mostly opposed to a fresh summons. After the
death of Louis XIV it was rumoured that the regent, the Duke of

42 *(Left)* The Estates-General of 1614, summoned in Paris by Marie de Médicis. It was the last to be summoned until 1789.

43 *(Right)* Assembly of notables held at Rouen in 1617. As a form of consultation, such assemblies proved as fractious and self-interested as the Estates-General, and no more helpful to government.

Orléans, was considering an assembly of the Estates-General, at the instigation of aristocratic reactionaries like the Ducs de Saint-Simon, Beauvillier, and Chevreuse, to 'restore' France as an aristocratic federation of provinces. Cardinal Dubois sent a memorandum to the regent imploring him not to commit such an act of folly. Shortly afterwards the *avocat général*, Lemoignon de Blancmenil, acting as a spokesman of one of the most formidable critics of the government, the *Parlement de Paris*, warned against summoning the Estates-General and declared: 'If the king were to be obliged to agree to their demands, he would cease to be king.' He voiced the opinions of many others besides himself.

The government did not at once despair after 1615 of using wide consultation to solve its problems. In 1617 and 1626 it summoned assemblies of notables. The meeting of 1626 was particularly well prepared by Cardinal Richelieu, for he badly needed money to pay the debts incurred in the recent civil wars and to enable him to intervene in the Thirty Years War against the Habsburgs. To this assembly were invited twelve prelates, ten nobles, and twenty-eight first presidents and *procureurs-généraux* of the *Parlements*. These dignitaries showed themselves as determined as the members of the Estates-General had been to defend the interests of their orders against the needs of the nation. Richelieu's attempt failed, and he and his successors realized that assemblies of notables were as unlikely to help their problems as the Estates-General had been.

The only representative assemblies left in France were the provincial Estates. A certain number of them, which had existed in the sixteenth century, fell into abeyance in the seventeenth. Such were the Estates of Auvergne, Rouergue, Périgord, Guienne, Dauphiné and Normandy. But this was not because of any active hostility on the part of the king; it was because the province in question was not sufficiently interested to want to keep the institution alive, in view of the time and cost involved. If a province was concerned enough, its orders remained united in defence of their privileges, and the leaders of provincial society acted with loyalty and moderation, the king was very content to respect such traditional rights. Indeed, when some Estates of tiny Pyrenean provinces were menaced by Colbert's mania for uniformity, they appealed to Louis XIV himself, and he intervened to save them. These provinces, usually on the periphery of the kingdom, where the sense of identity was strong, and where they were attached to their traditional privileges, kept their Estates until the Revolution. Such were Flanders, Artois, Brittany, Navarre, Béarn, Languedoc, Corsica, Burgundy and Provence.

If the Estates would co-operate with the Crown, then the king found them useful in smoothing the collection of taxes in the province and in assisting in its administration. To satisfy provincial feelings, the taxes from *pays d'état* were usually in the form of 'free gifts' (*dons gratuits*); but the Crown indicated what it needed, and expected taxation to keep roughly in step with that from the rest of France. The Estates met regularly: in Languedoc every year, in Brittany every two years, in Burgundy every three years. In Brittany and Burgundy eventually all nobles had the right to attend and sessions were often turbulent; in Languedoc the bishops took the lead and the proceedings were businesslike and decorous. The estates had permanent officers – *syndics*, treasurers, *greffiers* – who not only prepared the business, supervised taxation, and negotiated with the king and his officials, but sometimes (as in Brittany) sat in the provincial *Parlement* and supervised expenditure for public works in the province, such as canals and roads, and even the encouragement of letters and

44 The free *Reichstadt* or imperial town of Augsburg, in the sixteenth century.

the arts. It was generally agreed in the eighteenth century that the *pays d'état* were on the whole both more contented and better administered than the rest of France, and this was a large factor in the idealization of the provincial Estates on the eve of the Revolution and the demand for their extension to every province of the kingdom.

THE DECLINE OF THE LANDTAG

In Germany, too, the fortunes of the various Diets were not the same. The imperial parliament, the *Reichstag*, continued to exist but with diminishing authority. For a few years under Maximilian I at the end of the fifteenth century and again under Charles V in the 1520s, it looked as though the Kaiser might strengthen his authority. But these efforts were nullified by foreign entanglements and still more decisively by the dividing forces of the Reformation in the reign of Charles V. The Protestant princes resisted the power of the Kaiser on principle; the Catholic princes, like the dukes of Bavaria, took advantage of that opposition to weaken the emperor's authority over their own territories as well. From the end of the fifteenth century the *Reichstag* became more fully organized into three colleges: the *Kurfürsten* (electors), *Reichsfürsten* (imperial princes), and *Reichstädte* (imperial towns). The last two developed their internal organization, for example to arrange that lesser princes and towns combined to give one vote, whereas more important princes and towns had individual votes; and during recesses of the *Reichstag* the colleges carried on their activities through committees (*Reichsdeputationen*). The membership of the colleges became increasingly defined.

All these developments weakened the influence of the emperor. He found it increasingly difficult to add new members without opposition, or to gain consent to a tax on the empire as a whole. The sweeping victories of the imperial armies in the early stages of the Thirty Years War opened up for Ferdinand II visions of a grandiose revival of imperial authority. He began to add new members to the *Reichstag* at his pleasure (for example faithful Catholic Austrian noblemen), and to make new laws, such as the crucial Edict of Restitution in 1629, in consultation with only the Catholic electors. His military defeats in the 1630s put an end to such dreams. Even before the Treaty of Westphalia he was meeting with opposition in the *Reichstag* on questions such as majority decisions; that treaty struck a considerable blow to the Kaiser's authority in the *Reichstag* by admitting as members the Protestant administrators of secularized bishoprics. All that the emperor could do henceforth to counter this increase in the number of Protestant votes was to add only Catholic members whenever the opportunity offered.

But after 1648 it was plainly not worth while for the emperor to waste his energies over a body that represented a fatally weakened empire. The Emperor Leopold I tacitly recognized realities when, in 1663, he summoned the *Reichstag* and let it stay in permanent session, in which it was to remain until the dissolution of the empire in 1806. For it had become in effect a congress of delegates of virtually independent states which found it convenient to have a permanent centre for negotiation. They could cheerfully agree in 1667 to the rule of majority decisions, for henceforth the *Reichstag* would not normally dare to take action in decisive spheres such as the levying of taxes or raising of armies, and if it did take a disagreeable decision, this could usually be ignored with impunity. Authority had passed to the *Länder*.

Here the seventeenth century saw a striking decline in the power of the Diets in most German states. In a few the decline had already begun in the sixteenth century; in Bavaria, for example, the marked support for the Reformation in the Estates caused the Catholic dukes to rally all the forces of the Counter-Reformation to defeat them, a battle which the dukes were already winning by the end of the century. During the seventeenth century the power of the Estates waned still further, especially during the Thirty Years War, when Maximilian I used his large army to rule by decree and by arbitrary taxation. It is significant that after 1612 the Diet was not summoned for fifty-seven years; and the meeting of 1669 was to be the last in the history of the Bavarian *Landtag*. After that, until the end of the eighteenth century, only the standing committee of the *Landtag* (*die Verordnung*) met twice a year, to exercise the functions of the *Landtag* in taxation and financial administration. In Bavaria, as in many other parts of Germany, the devastations of the Thirty Years War had weakened both the nobility and the towns, and made it much more difficult to resist the prince if he had an efficient army.

The most striking case of such a development was that of Brandenburg. There the estates had been powerful in the fifteenth century, but the towns had lost much strength by economic developments and by the havoc caused by the war. The landed nobility had gained in judicial, social, and economic power and the Great Elector, recognizing realities, was willing to confirm and indeed strengthen this power in return for the junkers' help in his administration and his army. So, in spite of a struggle with his Estates, he got them to vote a sum of 530,000 thalers, which he used to raise a peacetime army that was never disbanded. With it he began to make Brandenburg's power felt in foreign affairs, and at home he used it to collect further taxes without the consent of the Estates, which by the end of the seventeenth century had fallen into disuse. And as the rulers of Brandenburg-Prussia gradually achieved ever more power, both at home and in Europe, the example of what they had done to the Estates became a potent influence in Germany. There was the even more dazzling example of Louis XIV to make absolutism seem attractive and the summoning of Estates appear old-fashioned and obstructive to efficient government. The *Landtag* disappeared in the Rhine Palatinate in the seventeenth century; in Baden-Durlach the last Diet was held in 1668 and in the duchy of Holstein the Diet met for the last time in 1675.

Yet the decline of the *Landtag* in the German principalities, though predominant, was not universal. Even in Prussia, the Estates continued a vigorous existence in Cleves and Mark, which had quite a different social structure and economic development from Germany east of the Elbe. They had to give up their right to negotiate with foreign powers, to exclude electoral troops, and to appoint and

45 *(Left)* The crown of Prussia, placed on the head of Frederick I in 1701.

46 *(Opposite)* Augustus the Strong, Elector of Saxony and King of Poland.

dismiss all officials, but they kept the privileges, all through the eighteenth century, of assembling when they wished and of voting their own taxes.

In Mecklenburg the Estates remained so strong that more than once they successfully appealed to the emperor and the Aulic Council against the attempts of the duke to levy taxes without their consent; and they successfully affirmed the unusual claim that the duke was himself subject to taxation. After a fresh appeal to the Aulic Council in 1755 an hereditary treaty (*Erbvergleich*) was made, which confirmed all the old privileges of the Estates – the powers of their officials and their Small Committee, their right to meet freely, their control over taxation. This treaty remained in force until 1918, long after the old constitutions of other German principalities had vanished.

In Württemberg, too, the Estates clashed with successive dukes, who wanted an increasingly large standing army, supported by taxation without consent. When Duke Charles Alexander (1733–37) became a convert to Roman Catholicism and gained administrative and military aid from other Catholic princes, it seemed that the Protestant Estates were doomed. But Charles died suddenly in 1737, the Estates hit back against his minions, and his successor made the error of appealing to Louis XV of France for support. After the defeat of France in the Seven Years War, this gave the *Landtag* the chance to

appeal to the Emperor Francis, and to Great Britain, Denmark and Prussia, to guarantee the constitution. As a result the duke was forced to conclude in 1770 an hereditary treaty which recognized the ancient privileges of the Estates and restored the constitution.

It was not only in secular principalities in Germany that Estates continued to exist. Even in the eighteenth century working representative institutions continued to function in many ecclesiastical principalities: in the electorates of Trier and Cologne and the bishoprics of Liège, Münster, Paderborn, Osnabrück, Hildesheim and Salzburg. These principalities had no hereditary dynasties, anxious to increase their power and to make war; no ecclesiastical principality initiated a war in the eighteenth century. The cathedral chapters, which formed the first estates in the north-west Church lands and in Salzburg, were both powerful and conservative. They examined the proposals of the princes before the Diet opened and they shared in the control of the armed forces. The canons usually occupied the most important government offices, and formed the government when the see was vacant. They were able to use their considerable influence in favour of the continued existence of the Diets, which were supported by the knights (from whom the canons were recruited) and the towns, such as Liège, Münster, Paderborn, Osnabrück, and Salzburg, which valued their importance there.

But even if it is true that many assemblies of estates survived in Germany to the French Revolution and beyond, it was absolute monarchy which enjoyed prestige in the seventeenth and eighteenth centuries. The defeat and disappearance of the Estates in Brandenburg-Prussia was associated with the spectacular rise to power of that state. In the Austrian dominions the Estates, usually dominated by the nobility, had been the centres of Protestant resistance to the centralizing Catholicism of the Habsburg monarchy. The imperialist victories in the early stages of the Thirty Years War gave the Counter-Reformation in the Austrian dominions its decisive advantage. Not only in Bohemia, but in Upper, Lower, and Inner Austria, the numerous Protestants were offered the choice of conversion or exile; and resistance could be crushed by the standing army that the monarchy had gained from the Thirty Years War. Protestantism had been strong in the towns and among the nobility, so the crushing of Protestantism had for the Habsburg monarchy the added attraction of crippling the power of the Estates.

47 The Empress Maria Theresa
wearing the crown of Hungary.

HUNGARY, THE IRELAND OF THE HABSBURGS

Protestantism was still strong in Hungary, not only in the Lutheran but also in the more militant Calvinist form, especially among the nobility, who were probably the most intractable subjects in Europe. As Hungary was reconquered by the Austrians from the Turks in the generation after the great siege of Vienna in 1683, the devout Emperor Leopold I tried hard, with alternating terror and persuasion, to turn Hungary, like Bohemia, into a Catholic and obedient province of the Habsburg monarchy. His grip on Hungary, in face of Turkish and French counter-attacks, was never strong enough to enable him to achieve this aim; but the attempt, made against a traditionally inde-pendent-minded nobility, only succeeded in arousing flaming resistance, which turned Hungary into the Ireland of the Habsburg monarchy. Even more than before, the Diet became the legal means and the symbol of Hungarian resistance. Hence the Habsburgs called it only rarely in the seventeenth century, and by-passed it in the eighteenth century. They summoned it only when a reign of terror had manifestly failed, and had led to violent Magyar resistance. This happened for example in 1681, when Leopold I gave back to the Magyars their rights of self-government, offered to call off the perse-cution of Protestants, and promised that the Diet was to meet every three years. It is true that by 1687 Leopold was sufficiently master of Hungary to try to whittle down the liberties he had granted in 1681; but his policy of conciliation in 1681 was just in time to ensure that most Hungarians did not join in the great attack of the Turks on Vienna in 1683.

The same policy of conciliation in difficult days for the monarchy paid a handsome dividend in 1741, when the youthful Maria Theresa, faced with nothing less than the break-up of her empire under the

111

joint attacks of the Prussians, Bavarians and French, appealed to the chivalrous instincts of the Magyar nobility by appearing in person at the Diet of Pozsony with her baby son Joseph in her arms. But though she was intelligent, wise and humane, to her and her reforming minister Kaunitz and her radical son Joseph the Hungarian Diet seemed the turbulent expression of a restless, ungovernable people, an obstacle in its prejudiced conservatism to rational, efficient, enlightened government. Something was achieved by cajoling some of the leading families, like the Esterhazys, Rakoczis and Karolyis, to become Germanized and Catholic, in return for important executive posts. But Hungary remained one of the most limited monarchies in Europe; for even if the Diet were managed or out-manœuvred, there were still the county Diets, which passed local laws and elected executive officials. The Hungarian aristocracy might at times be won over in Buda or Vienna; but the lesser nobility dominated the counties, and they were too numerous, too Magyar in tradition, habits and speech, too independent in spirit, to be suborned or intimidated. They constituted the real and formidable resistance to Habsburg absolutism.

Nevertheless, by the late seventeenth century it was possible for most governments and many advanced thinkers to regard Estates as archaic obstacles to efficient government and state power, to consider Diets as tiresome defenders of class and regional privileges, of antiquated procedures and out-of-date customs. If the nobility was firmly entrenched, if local sentiment remained strong, if the government was traditionalist in outlook and sluggish in spirit, then the assemblies of estates might continue with diminished use and importance. Such was the case in the Austrian monarchy, not only in recalcitrant Hungary but even in the Austrian provinces and Bohemia. But if governments had the chance, they often seized their opportunity to let the Estates fall into disuse. Thus in Italy by the beginning of the eighteenth century, apart from very minor assemblies, the only parliaments still meeting were those in the March of Ancona, the Venetian province of Friuli, and the Spanish-controlled Sicily; of these only the Sicilian parliament was still of much importance. The last session of the parliament of the kingdom of Naples had taken place in 1642, and the last session of the Sardinian parliament was held in 1698. Sometimes the end came, not gently by mere abeyance, but abruptly – either because of rebellion, as in Aragon in 1707 and 1714, or because of defeat in war, as happened in Denmark in 1660.

The Danish Crown had benefited from the confiscations of Church lands at the Reformation, and the hitherto powerful Church had been subdued, not only by its loss of lands, but by its subjugation to royal authority. But at the same time the nobility had gained in power. As in England, it managed to share considerably in the plunder of Church lands, and social forces were thrusting down the once free peasantry into serfdom. In medieval times the Danish kings had often been almost puppets in the hands of nobles and clergy, and the monarchy still had a long way to go before it could direct the government without control or interference. The *Rigsdag* (or Diet) and even more the *Rigsraad* (or Council) had to be constantly consulted in the levy of taxation and the conduct of affairs. In both these bodies the nobles enjoyed increased power after the Reformation. From the meetings of the *Rigsdag* the peasants were disappearing as they sank into serfdom, and the clergy had no longer the independent role that they had once enjoyed. From the *Rigsraad* the bishops had vanished, leaving the nobles in control. They maintained their tradition of exercising a check on the king in the conduct of affairs, even claiming to decide whether his acts were legal. As a consequence they reaped the odium of the striking defeats and humiliation of Christian IV when he tried to be the Protestant champion in the early stages of the Thirty Years War. The clergy and the towns were especially bitter about this. Henceforward the Council had to be much more humble; but the large powers of the *Rigsdag*, especially in finance, still remained.

The *Rigsdag* in turn was blamed for the humiliating Swedish invasions of Denmark in the war of 1658–60. In 1658 and 1659 the king, Frederick III, was the hero of the resistance of Copenhagen against the alarming onslaughts of the Swedes, declaring to the admiring citizens that he would die in his own nest. If, in the Peace of Oliva in 1660, Denmark suffered the further humiliation of the loss of the ancient and fertile Danish province of Skåne (Scania) to the Swedes, bringing them almost within sight of Copenhagen, it was not the heroic king who was blamed by public opinion in Denmark. It was the *Rigsdag*, and in particular the nobility, whose selfish opposition to the efficient conduct of the war had endangered the very independence of the country. Both clergy and townsmen were eager for constitutional reform, and the nobility was too stunned by the shock of defeat to resist. The Diet adopted the principle of hereditary monarchy in place of the previously crippling elective principle. The king was released from his previous engagements, and the three estates remitted to him the power to reform the government as he should think best. On 18 October 1660, the king received the homage of the estates as an hereditary monarch, and they dispersed, confident that they would soon be meeting again. They were in fact not to reassemble for another 175 years. Until the mid-nineteenth century the kings of Denmark, in striking contrast to their predecessors, were amongst the most absolute rulers in Europe. This did not, of course, save a small country from all troubles; but it is significant that until the nineteenth century there was no strong movement in Denmark for constitutional government. Absolute government, for all its imperfections, seemed to most Danes preferable to the power of the *Rigsdag* and the *Rigsraad* in the preceding era.

There was one striking instance where defeat in war worked the other way, the case of Sweden after the disasters and death of Charles XII. Sweden was unusual in its parliamentary history in various ways. In the early seventeenth century, when many parliaments were under pressure from their monarchies, Gustavus Adolphus was making increased use of the *Riksdag* in his government. Feeling that the Swedes were insufficiently united or politically aware, he made it a recognized custom to give accounts to the *Riksdag* of the political situation. By taking the nation into partnership, he hoped to induce the *Riksdag* to vote more promptly and adequately the taxes that he must have for his military forces, large for such a sparsely peopled country. He wanted prompt decisions and therefore tried to insist that the representatives should come to the *Riksdag* with full powers, and not seek to refer problems to the provinces. He also enhanced the status of the *Riksdag* for his own purposes by insisting that any taxes it voted must be recognized by all as having the full authority of law.

From the monarchy's point of view he succeeded only too well in raising the prestige and importance of the *Riksdag*. The different estates came to value the debates and the powers of the assembly, and to gain confidence in refusing sometimes the apparently endless demands of the monarchy for wars. Gustavus had insisted in 1626 on the attendance at the *Riksdag* of every noble above fifteen years of age, on full representation of the clergy through bishops and representatives of cathedral chapters and parishes, and on two burgesses for each town down to quite small units. This made the orders of the

48 *(Above)* Frederick III of Denmark acknowledged as hereditary monarch in 1660. The *Rigsdag* was extinguished for 175 years, and absolutism took over.

49 *(Right)* Gustavus Adolphus of Sweden. By taking the *Riksdag* into his confidence he aimed to involve the nation in the process of government.

Riksdag all the more effectively the representatives of the nation, especially as it continued (unlike the Danish *Rigsdag*) to contain representatives of the peasantry as well.

By the late seventeenth century, however, the kings became impatient of their dependence on the *Riksdag*, and of its claims. Between 1680 and 1682 Charles XI tried to make himself more independent financially by restoring to the Crown any property alienated from the state in the past without any time-limit, and ruled that in matters of legislation he was not bound to have the approval of the *Riksdag*. He was allowed to have his way in these measures because of the brilliant record of the Vasa kings on behalf of Sweden and because of the pressing needs of the monarchy in the perilous situation of the 1680s. Moreover, the non-noble estates had become jealous of the power which the nobles had acquired through their role in the armies of the Crown since the days of Gustavus Adolphus. But the resumption of lands by the Crown caused a growing resentment among the nobility, a resentment at first kept in check by the success of the peace policy of Charles XI and then by the dazzling victories in war of his son Charles XII. The young Charles XII, more imperious and rash than his father, declared himself an autocrat at his accession in 1697, and placed the crown on his own head. During his amazing reign the acts of his government were carried out on the strength of his orders or those of his officials. But even his military genius was insufficient to win permanent success with the resources of a small and increasingly exhausted country against a circle of foreign foes, including the Russia of Peter the Great. After his death in Norway in 1718 there was a great reaction in Sweden. Autocracy was thought to have brought the country to disaster and exhaustion, so in the constitution of 1720 power was transferred from the king to the revived *Riksdag*.

During the next fifty years, the 'Age of Liberty', as it was known in Swedish history, the king was hardly more than the president of the Council which was appointed by the *Riksdag* and had to report to it at each meeting. Any member of the Council (*Riksråd*) who did not satisfy the political demands of the *Riksdag* could be removed by it. Thus the *Riksdag* of the Age of Liberty was one of the most powerful representative assemblies that has ever existed; and its Secret Committee (*Sekreta Utskottet*), to which nearly all important matters were referred, was virtually the ruler of the state, even against the king. So

50 A seventeenth-century Swedish medal shows the four orders represented in the *Riksdag*: the nobility, the clergy, the burgesses and the peasants – effectively the representatives of the nation.

powerful were the members of the *Riksdag* and the Secret Committee that the ambassadors of foreign governments in Stockholm had funds to try to secure a majority in either body. For it was soon discovered that members could be bribed, either by promotion or favours for themselves or their supporters, or by the manipulation of the subsidies paid to encourage various industries. Rival parties sought to control the levers of power. For over twenty-five years the party of the Hats was in command, and neither failures in foreign policy nor the feeble plots of King Adolphus Frederick and Queen Louisa Ulrica could shake their power. Eventually the Swedish reverses in the Seven Years War and the mounting corruption swept them out of power in the *Riksdag* of 1765–66 in favour of their rivals, the Caps. These claimed to be in favour of more open and honest methods of government; they abolished the Secret Committee, the censorship, and subsidies to industries. But their economic policy was unsuccessful and their policy of subservience to Russia was felt to be humiliating. The development of prosperity and education among the commoners caused resentment at the privileges and the dominance of the nobles in the *Riksdag*.

In alarm, some of the nobility began to look to the impotent Crown as a desirable ally, to be made more potent to defend their privileges. In this situation, the position of the Crown was greatly improved by the death in 1771 of the ineffective King Adolphus Frederick and the accession of his able and vigorous son Gustavus III. He had only to wait a few months to let the parties in the *Riksdag* discredit themselves

51 *(Overleaf)* The coronation of Gustavus III of Sweden, in the presence of representatives of the four estates. Less than a year later, Gustavus had taken sole power into his own hands.

still further by their quarrels and self-seeking; then in August 1772 he was able to stage a *coup d'état* without any opposition. The hitherto proud estates listened in silence to Gustavus's new constitution, which aimed to return to the days of Gustavus Adolphus and to leave undefined the rights of the estates to tax and to legislate. The *Riksdag* was then sent away for six years, and Gustavus was able to start his career as an enlightened despot. It is true that his restless foreign policies and his eventual attack on the privileges of the nobility combined to lead to his assassination in 1792 by a group of disgruntled nobles. Nevertheless, it is significant that at the time of his *coup d'état* Gustavus was widely applauded, both in Sweden and elsewhere in western Europe, as having performed an intelligent, progressive act.

In 1772 this seemed a very reasonable point of view to educated and up-to-date people. Had not Frederick the Great by his autocratic power and wise devotion to the state made his country the greatest military power in Europe, and yet fostered both industry and agriculture after an especially devastating war? Could not Catherine the Great already claim to be using her despotic authority for the promotion of the prosperity of Russia, the modernization of its laws, the civilizing of its manners and mode of life? In Austria was not Joseph II, in spite of his mother's misgivings, waging war against error, traditionalism, superstition, and all the other enemies of human progress? Would the Austrian empire ever exploit its vast resources to the full and regain its rightful position in Europe if all the irrational obstacles of language, religion, class, custom, and local prejudice were not overcome? And who was more likely to do this – an enlightened despot, or assemblies of estates which were the very defenders of such irrational obstacles? In Denmark the rise of Struensee had been offensive to aristocratic sentiment; the elevation of the son of a pastor to the position of chief minister and virtual dictator, and his relations with the queen, affronted their prejudices and explain his fall and execution. But what rational man could deny that his spate of Cabinet orders had been designed to make the Danes prosperous and happy? Would the *Rigsdag* have achieved as much – or even attempted it?

THE IMPOTENT CORTES

Perhaps the most impressive example of what could be achieved by enlightened despotism was taking place in Spain. In that unhappy land the decline had been so profound during the seventeenth and early

52 *(Left)* Allegorical drawing in praise of the Emperor Joseph II's reform of the Church. Under the all-seeing eye of Heaven the Emperor promises the money-grubbing clerics, 'from now on you will be fishers of men'.

53 *(Right)* Charles III of Spain, an enlightened despot who did all he could to lessen the nobles' grip on the machinery of government.

eighteenth centuries that observers wondered whether she could ever recover from the long series of military defeats, the abject poverty of the masses, the lethargy, the inefficiency, and the misgovernment. Who could possibly cope with the almost pathological preoccupation with *hidalguía* (nobility) and *limpieza de sangre* (purity of blood), the disdain for business and manual occupations, the special privileges of the grandees, the growing abyss between the rich and noble few and the poverty-stricken masses, the enormous numbers of the clergy (about 200,000), the absence of an enterprising bourgeoisie, the fatalistic acceptance of constant death and disaster, the pervasion of the government machinery by the nobility, the crippling effects of the sale of offices, the formidable local powers of grandees on their vast estates? And yet Charles III and his ministers were making an impact, in a more cautious way than Joseph II in Austria, and bringing back some modest prosperity to Spain's wasted body. Were they not making an energetic effort (more cautiously, it was true, since the Mutiny of Esquilache in 1766) to improve the efficiency of administration at all levels, to lessen the grip of the nobility and the Church on education, the administration and the economy, to reduce the blighting influence of the Inquisition, to encourage practical and economic development, to help the agriculture of Castile and the nascent industries and commerce of Catalonia? Could anything have been expected of the *Cortes*?

In 1789, of all years, the first business to be discussed by the *Cortes* of Spain after the official opening was the requests of the deputies from Burgos; one of these was a supplication for good seats at the forthcoming bullfight. The towns represented in the *Cortes* were dominated by a traditionalist outlook as strong as that of the grandees or the Inquisition. Until the reign of Charles III they were represented by noble oligarchs without question; and though he and his ministers tried to introduce a democratic element into town government by the election of *diputados*, the *diputados* themselves tried to convert their temporary representation of the people into a life office and so to become ennobled. The *Cortes* was as yet too much part of the old traditional society to promote any reforms. Enlightened thinkers stressed the duty of the ruler to act in a wide range of affairs to benefit the whole state, and held that rational, uniform means should be used to that end. Would the eighteenth-century *Cortes* assist in, or even understand, such aims?

POLAND OF THE NOBLES

Few of the surviving Diets in Europe were likely to impress a supporter of enlightened despotism in 1772. He might have conceded that in Spain, France, Italy or Austria they served a useful function in easing the levy of taxation, under the guidance of the government; though he might have added that it would make for more efficient administration if they could be phased out. But where assemblies of estates exercised real authority in the government of the state, he might have been excused for thinking that they were usually a drag on good and smooth government. Apart from Sweden, where Gustavus III carried out his *coup d'état* in this year, such an observer might well have considered Poland a particularly telling example of the evils of

54 The election of Stanislas Poniatowski as King of Poland in 1764. The king was elected by the whole of the nobility, and the balance of power was weighted heavily against the Crown.

government by Diets. There the balance of power had already been shifting from monarchy to nobility in the fifteenth century, and in the sixteenth the shift became decisive. The gain in the social power of the nobility was shown by the series of laws passed by the Diet between 1496 and 1541 subjecting the peasantry to seignorial courts, denying access to royal courts, and tying them to the soil. Most towns were subjected to noble administrators, all but a few towns lost their representation in the Diet, and even these few had no votes. By the end of the century the deputies of towns and of cathedral chapters disappeared entirely from the *Sejm*.

From 1573 onwards the king was elected by the whole of the nobility, on the basis of a contract which he had to swear not to break. Thenceforward the nobles had the right to refuse obedience if the king did not respect his engagements. In 1578 the royal court was replaced as the supreme court of justice by the Tribunal of the Crown, elected annually by the nobility, and for some offices the king could only appoint candidates presented by the Diet. In the second half of the sixteenth century there triumphed the concept of the 'noble nation', from which burgesses and peasants were excluded. Nobility became such a precious jewel that from 1578 the king had to gain the consent of the Diet for the conferment of nobility, and from 1669 the decision had to be unanimous. Moreover, the nobles were determined not to allow the slightest reduction in their privileges, for this might lead to absolute monarchy, and in the seventeenth century the principle of unanimity began to be applied more and more rigorously in the Diet. Because of the veto, between 1652 and 1764 no less than fifty-three Diets dispersed without passing any laws. The king, with his counsellors and government officials, was subject to the will of the biennial Diet, without whose consent no important decision might be taken. The king still appointed the officials of the land, but they were irremovable, both in law and in practice.

Ironically, the completeness of the victory of the Diet hastened its impotence. In the increasingly anarchical condition into which Poland was fast slipping in the seventeenth century the greater nobility, the magnates, gained at the expense of the lesser; and the magnates were not going to be frustrated in their ambitions by a Diet subject to the veto of the poorest gentleman. Exultant in its legislative power, the Diet began to act as a supreme court to quash sentences imposed by the Tribunal. Again, this speeded its decline.

Were the magnates, whose influence was predominant in the Tribunal, to see their cases at risk in a Diet where swarms of small nobility sat? The magnates preferred to work through the regional Diets, the dietines, usually dominated by the aristocratic faction with the biggest landed estates in that region. Through the dietine the magnate could raise troops (ostensibly for the king but usually for himself) and levy taxes (on the lower orders only, of course). The troops were raised and the taxes collected by stewards elected in the dietines but in fact chosen by the magnate from lesser nobility who were his clients. If all else failed, the magnates could declare a confederacy for the achievement of a common political aim and take up arms in defence of it, theoretically in the name of the king but usually against him.

It is not surprising that Poland was devastated by almost continual warfare, both internal and foreign; of the seventy years between 1648 and 1717 fifty-five were years of war, hunger, fire and plague. In these circumstances the powers of the magnates increased. The population shrank by a third, and by the late eighteenth century the export of grain was about one-third of what it had been in the early seventeenth century. This was from a country increasingly agricultural; for the state of the towns was so bad that most artisans had to take to agriculture and leave the Jews to act as the agents of the great landlords in buying and selling at their privileged rates. Trade and industry were on the point of extinction, and the peasantry sank into ever deeper subjection and misery. By the end of the seventeenth century Poland had become in effect a federation of territories in which political life developed chiefly in the châteaux of the magnates. The king sank to the position of merely one of the more important of the contestants in the constant armed struggles between the leading families, especially that between the Potockis and the Czartoryskis. In these circumstances it was very hard for the king to avoid total impotence. If he tried, as Augustus II did in 1719, with the support of Austria and Hanover against Russia, to carry out constitutional reform, he found the deputies determined not to do anything that might involve the country in another war or increase the powers of the Crown.

This was probably the last chance of salvation. Thenceforward Russia and Prussia began to contemplate dismemberment of Poland when the time should be ripe, as can be seen from the repeated actions and statements of the rulers of those two countries, from the Treaty

of Potsdam in 1720 onwards. The shock of the First Partition of 1772 caused the Poles to attempt reforms, and from 1773 onwards a permanent council of thirty-six, with large powers, was chosen by the *Sejm* to advise the king, thus avoiding the paralysis of action familiar under the old magnate officers of state. In 1791 the Poles astonished Europe by their bloodless revolution, when in May the king and the Patriots persuaded the Diet to accept a new constitution with an hereditary monarchy, a strong executive, a national legislature, and renunciation of privilege and of the veto. This merely precipitated the Second and Third Partitions and the extinction of Poland as an independent state. The example of Poland as a state dominated by its Diet had not been a happy one.

55 (*Opposite*) Count Potocki, by Jacques-Louis David. The Potockis and the Czartoryskis were two of the leading families whose violent rivalries fatally weakened Poland and led to her partition.

56 (*Above*) The abdication of Charles V, 1555: even before the revolt against Spain, the States-General were sufficiently important for the king to take official leave of them.

RISE AND FALL OF THE HOUSE OF ORANGE

Less repellent but not widely inviting was the case of the Netherlands, controlled since the revolt against Spain by its States-General. After the Southern Netherlands had fallen to the armies of Farnese in 1579, the States-General of the Spanish Netherlands was only summoned again twice by the Spaniards, in 1598 and 1632. On both occasions the Spanish government was alienated by its quarrelling and its obstinacy, and after 1632 it never met again until the national agitation against Joseph II's attempts at enlightened reforms in 1790. But in the United Provinces the resistance to Philip II had been initiated on the authority of the States-General, and it was this body which, in July 1581, issued the Act of Abjuration of allegiance to Philip II. The States-General claimed that after this the sovereignty of the provinces had reverted to itself. Efforts to find a new king all failed, and the Netherlands settled down to a republican form of government. William the Silent, and other members of his House after him, had played a glorious part in the War of Liberation; but in origin they were simply Netherlands nobles, and their authority had to be exercised in the name of the States-General, either as *Stadhouder* (governor) or as commander-in-chief, or both. The States-General had supreme control of military and naval matters and foreign affairs. It appointed the captain-general and admiral-general of the Union, and a deputation of the States-General went with the army into the field, to be consulted by the commanders. The States-General supervised finance, and administered the 'Generality' lands.* It appointed the treasurer-general of the Union, the ambassadors, and numerous other important officials. To foreigners indeed the sovereignty of the United Netherlands appeared to be vested in the members of the States-General, who were officially addressed as 'Your High Mightinesses'.

In reality, however, the States-General was only a gathering of deputations from seven sovereign provinces. In all important questions – foreign affairs, finance, peace and war – there must be no dissentient. Each province voted as a unit, and the smallest province could therefore block any proposal if it chose to be obstinate. The deputation of each province was given most careful instructions each time it set out for The Hague, and if any matter should arise on which the deputies had not been briefed, they had to refer back to the Estates of their province for instructions as to how to act. Hence there were countless opportunities and reasons for dissension, obstruction, and delays in reaching decisions about the affairs of the Republic, sometimes on vital matters. To make matters worse, the president of the States-General changed each week, being chosen in turn from each province according to their order of precedence; and this could happen even when the government was coping with a crisis, such as an invasion. Moreover, Holland, as much the richest province, was

* These were the conquests from Brabant, Limburg and Flanders, which belonged to none of the seven United Provinces separately and had therefore to be administered by the States-General.

57 *(Left)* The States-General of the United Netherlands assembled in the Great Hall of the Binnenhof, 1651. 58 *(Right)* The Binnenhof ('inner courtyard'), The Hague.

apt to take an independent line; in spite of the terms of the Union, it sometimes refused (as in 1638) to acknowledge the authority of the States-General to impose taxes on it, or even (as in 1648) ventured to negotiate direct with foreign powers. As the province of Holland contributed 57·1 per cent of the quotas for the army, and even more for the navy, such an independent spirit was a serious matter. Indeed, one of the reasons why the King of Spain made large concessions in 1609 to secure a twelve years' truce was the firm belief in Spain that such an absurd method of government must lead to civil strife as soon as the unifying bond of war had been removed.

There were, of course, to be quarrels, such as the famous one between Maurice and Oldenbarneveldt in 1618–19; but the United Netherlands, far from disintegrating, went forward to the most glorious century of its history. This was because there were many unifying forces not apparent in the constitution. The very preponderance of Holland meant that time and again its influence (and especially that of wealthy and populous Amsterdam) carried the day. The States-General was very small, consisting of only twenty-four men (the number who could sit round the Council table at the

Binnenhof in The Hague), so that they came to know each other intimately. Nearly all of them were drawn from the same tiny class of regent burghers, the small patrician oligarchies of Calvinist allegiance in whose hands the entire government of the towns was concentrated; and even if they differed on particular measures, they shared the same fundamental outlook, interests, and way of life.

In addition there was that fortunate anomaly for a republic, the office of *Stadhouder* or governor in each province, a survival from Burgundian and Habsburg rule. William the Silent had been *Stadhouder* of Holland and Zeeland; such was his prestige as 'father of his country' that, on his death, his son Maurice was soon made *Stadhouder* in his stead. Such was Maurice's brilliance as both soldier and statesman that he became *Stadhouder* of Utrecht, Gelderland, and Overijssel as well, in addition to being captain-general and admiral-general of the Union. His equally brilliant brother Frederick Henry was appointed to all these offices after his brother's death, and became in addition *Stadhouder* of Groningen and head of the Council of State. In 1631 the States-General voted to make these offices hereditary in his son William II. Since the *Stadhouder* was the executive officer of the Estates of his province, this conjunction of offices enabled the Prince of Orange to act (if he placated the States-General) as the head and representative of the Union. This role was strengthened by the facts that the remaining governorship, that of Friesland, was in the hands of always faithful cousins, and that the Princes of Orange had enough wealth to enable them to maintain the dignity of a court.

The autocratic behaviour of William II, followed by his sudden death in 1650 at the age of twenty-four, leaving no heir, encouraged the republican oligarchs of Holland to abolish the governorship of that province and to persuade the States-General to declare that no *Stadhouder* could hold either the captain- or admiral-generalship of the Union. But the Netherlands were not Poland, where swarms of nobles and proud magnates could long think themselves secure in their vast plains, behind marshes and rivers. No Dutchman could forget the desperate sacrifices needed for the birth and survival of his country, the absolute necessity of unity in face of foreign invasion, and the glorious role of the House of Orange. So when, in 1672, Louis XIV launched his sudden attack and overran two-thirds of the Netherlands in a few months, there was overwhelming popular acclamation of William III, the posthumous son of William II. This

59 Patrician Dutch burgher regents of the early eighteenth century.

young man of twenty-one was rapidly elected *Stadhouder* of six provinces, captain- and admiral-general; and his leading opponents, the de Witt brothers, were murdered in The Hague by Orange mobs. For the rest of his life William III, more tactful than his father, never failed to gain the support of the States-General in his great struggle against Louis XIV, even though it constantly involved both courage and great sacrifices.

For four generations the House of Orange had produced great leaders; but William III, the greatest of them all, left no successor save a distant cousin, a boy of fourteen. By reason of family tradition he succeeded as *Stadhouder* in Friesland and Groningen, but the other provinces reverted to a republican form of government. In 1746, during the War of the Austrian Succession, the French overran Belgium and threatened the Netherlands. Popular resentment against the feebleness and corruption of the republican government was intense. As in 1672 there was an irresistible clamour for the Prince of Orange to save the country; and in 1747 not only did the States-General make the offices of captain- and admiral-general hereditary in the House of Orange, but every province made the dignity of *Stadhouder* hereditary in the descendants of William IV, in both the male and female lines.

To some extent the lack of a firm executive authority in the Netherlands was now remedied; and by the 1780s the Orange-*Stadhouder* party and the patrician-regent party, which had been so often at loggerheads in the past, inside and outside the States-General, drew together (except in Holland) in face of the rising democratic or 'patriot' party, which wanted to abolish all privileges in Church and state and to proclaim the sovereignty of the people.

Nevertheless, foreign observers were not impressed by the Netherlands' system of government, and there was no desire to import it. From the point of view of the enlightened despot, it was neither efficient nor centralizing nor progressive. The great achievements of the seventeenth century had been effected almost in spite of the defects of the States-General, and in the eighteenth century the decline of the Netherlands in power and prestige had been hastened by the inertia, timidity and corruption of the patrician class, growing more exclusive with each generation, reigning supreme as a small exclusive oligarchy over their towns and the surrounding countryside. For those whose political ideas were inspired by Rousseau, the constitution was just as defective: it consisted of a large number of semi-independent oligarchies of the narrowest type, and the great mass of the population had no civic rights at all. By the late 1780s the government was so feeble that when, in 1787, Holland came under tumultuous patriot control, *Stadhouder* William V and his Prussian wife had no other recourse but to appeal for support to the British and Prussian governments. Prussian armed force and English diplomatic support succeeded in restoring the authority of the hereditary *Stadhouder* and the States-General, but that authority was now seen to be dependent on foreign support. When in 1795 the French invaded the country and proclaimed the revolutionary Batavian Republic, the guardians of the old constitution, both *Stadhouder* William V and the patrician oligarchies, offered no resistance at all.

In the two generations before the French Revolution there was in fact only one parliamentary institution which aroused enthusiasm in other lands. This was the British Parliament, which became especially admired in France. It was a remarkable change of opinion from that of two or three generations earlier. In the later seventeenth century the English methods of government seemed to Frenchmen a warning of how not to run a nation's affairs. Had not the English Parliament murdered one king, expelled another, flouted the divine right of kings, and caused repeated obstruction and faction in the affairs of the state? After the execution of Charles I in 1649 a merchant at Nantes had had to beg a correspondent not to call him English, for in that case he would not be safe from lynching in the streets. In his memorandum of 1715 to the regent against the summoning of an Estates-General Cardinal Dubois pointed to the awful example of England, where, he said, the triumph of Parliament had obviously ruined both the Crown and true religion. To men who regarded the absolutism of Louis XIV as the model of political development such a view of the British Parliament was natural.

But the death of Louis XIV released a confused tide of criticism, which was to mount in strength during the long reign of his inadequate successor; the prestige of the British constitution and the British Parliament rose accordingly. The glory of absolute monarchy involved increasing expenditure on pomp, bureaucracy, pensions, and war, but it was founded on a woefully inadequate financial system which had already resulted in financial deficits that were to prove incurable. This not only meant an increasing burden of taxation for the unprivileged, but led to a financial crisis that ultimately precipitated the fall of the régime itself. But, as Frenchmen enviously observed, the British were able to wage war without ruining their country and their financial resources seemed inexhaustible. The British aristocracy played a more important and dignified part in the affairs of the state than the French nobility, even in the aristocratic resurgence of the reign of Louis XV; yet the British nobility made no claim to exemption from taxation, an exemption which in France was both a prime reason for the financial deficits and a cause for growing resentment by the unprivileged middle classes.

Furthermore, in spite of the efforts of Colbert and his successors to promote prosperity, French trade and industry were greatly hampered

60 *(Left)* French pre-revolutionary print: the peasant, bowed under the burden of taxation, is seen as supporting the clergy and nobility.

61 *(Opposite) Josiah Wedgwood and his Family* (1780), by George Stubbs: the *philosophes* believed England's prosperity to be the result of a more open system of government.

by internal tolls, customs, seigneurial dues, and octrois, and by the officially protected gilds. These restrictions on trade benefited only the numerous office-holders and members of the privileged classes, but for that very reason they were upheld, like other privileges, by the surviving provincial Estates, themselves composed of privileged persons. Again it was a matter of envy to reforming Frenchmen that English industry could be so free of such vexatious restrictions, and yet the British Parliament could with such ease impose extra tariffs or excise if the government deemed them necessary. As Montesquieu observed, the parliament of King, Lords and Commons had the power to make binding laws and correct errors. This gave a flexibility lacking in the Roman constitution, and it helped to explain the success of the British government. Moreover, as writers like Voltaire and Mirabeau pointed out, the British system managed to produce a government

strong enough to create and defend a great empire while France was losing hers; to encourage an economy so progressive that it was rapidly making the United Kingdom the most prosperous country in the world, and yet at the same time to allow a liberty to the subject that contrasted sharply with the oppressions of French law – its arbitrary arrests and imprisonment, its use of torture and the galleys, its persecution of heresy or free thought.

So for French reformers the British Parliament (viewed through rose-coloured spectacles) was a powerful encouragement, for it seemed to demonstrate that the aims of the *philosophes* were not only desirable but practicable. It was possible to have a representative assembly which co-operated in strong and effective government, which respected and upheld traditional institutions like the monarchy, the aristocracy, and the Church, yet protected the liberty of the subject

135

and the principle of equality before the law, and fostered the accumulation of wealth and the development of industry. As early as the *Voyage* of Sorbière (1669), the importance of the Lower House in the preservation and extension of parliamentary powers had been observed in France. In the eighteenth century, writers like De Lolme and Mirabeau noticed the importance of the plenipotentiary powers of the knights and burgesses, and of the fact that they represented communities of the shire and the borough, not merely the knights and the burgesses of the land. Thus the Commons could claim to speak for the nation. This could be, and increasingly was, interpreted to mean, in French terms, the third estate. Thus encouraged, the reformers joined the increasing clamour for the summons of the Estates-General, which, they believed, would cure the nation's ills. They were heartened by the success of the American Revolution, which had been an intoxicating victory for liberty and equality of status and had produced a better version of the British constitution.

But by 1789 the idea of summoning the Estates-General meant fundamentally different things to different groups of people. The differences were already apparent in the proposals for provincial Estates and provincial assemblies. The older concept had come from the group of friends of the Duke of Burgundy, heir apparent in 1711–12 – men like Fénélon, his tutor, and the Dukes of Beauvillier and Chevreuse. They had advocated the extension of the régime of provincial Estates to all parts of the realm, with governors instead of intendants. This implied a return to an idealized noble past, and reinforcement of the pre-eminence of the aristocracy and particularist feelings as they were thought to have been before Louis XIV had invented his centralized administration manned by 'vile bourgeoisie'. One of the group, Saint-Simon, extended this contempt of the third estate to the members of the *Parlements* who, though they had bought judicial offices, could never, he wrote, escape from their 'essential baseness'.

This was already archaic when it was written in 1716; and as the century advanced, the officials of the *Parlements* became increasingly part of the nobility, in status, habits, and outlook. They claimed to judge any royal edict or exercise of authority by the rule of law, and law meant for them the whole range of privileges as they then stood – the privileges of the princes of the blood, of the nobles, of the clergy, of the corporations of towns, and gilds, and officials, and universities,

62 Gaspard de Gueidan, President of the *Parlement de Paris*, playing the bagpipes: indisputably an aristocrat, in dress and hobby.

63 The provosts of Paris. By the eighteenth century, the representatives of towns were as deeply entrenched in their privileges as the nobility or clergy.

and provincial Estates. But by the end of the reign of Louis XV it was becoming clear that urgent and fundamental reforms like the reform of the tax and judicial systems could never be achieved without the abolition of privileges. The provincial Estates, as they stood, were bound up with the *ancien régime*; for not only were the nobles and clergy obviously privileged, but so were the representatives of the towns. They were usually members of an hereditary group, exempt from *taille*, eligible to acquire 'noble land', and frequently possessing prior rights for sale, a monopoly of dealing in their commodity, and exemption from tolls.

The second idea of representation was perhaps first expressed by D'Argenson in 1737 but owed its popularity to the physiocrats when, after 1756, it was taken up by men like Mirabeau, Turgot, and Dupont de Nemours. It was based on the Enlightenment notions that men were naturally good, that their individual interests coincided with the general interest, that originally they had been free and equal; for a society of orders and corporations there ought therefore to be sub-stituted the society of classes, an open society whose members, free and equal before the law, would be distinguished from one another only by fortune, by talents, and by way of life. As a means of attaining this end, and of remedying the ills from which France was suffering, there ought to be in every province, town, and community an assembly elected by property-owners, without distinction of orders; to this assembly would be entrusted the levy and distribution of taxation, the preparation of public works and the drawing up of proposals for reform.

In the increasingly desperate state of the finances in the 1780s, the ministers of Louis XVI were ready to clutch at any expedient which seemed at all likely to alleviate the growing debts; might not the proposed provincial assemblies come up with new ideas of taxation? So in June 1787 the principal minister, Archbishop Loménie de Brienne, issued an edict setting up provincial and municipal assemblies in all regions where there were no provincial Estates. Like Necker before him, who had experimented on a small scale with this idea, Brienne was too timid to go the whole way with the physiocrats, and the provincial assemblies were to be composed of representatives of the nobility, the clergy, and the third estate. But the new ideas had made sufficient impact to cause him to give double representation to the third estate and to decree that the assembly would meet together, not in separate estates, and that the voting would be by head and not by order. These provisions, together with that for election by taxpayers of ten francs or more, would ensure the dominance of the unprivileged small proprietors.

The *Parlements* of Paris, Besançon, Grenoble, and Bordeaux fiercely denounced these assemblies as 'unconstitutional'. On the other hand, the sympathies of the unprivileged were alienated by two blunders. Firstly, the government said that it was impossible to arrange elections before 1790, so for the assemblies of 1787 the king nominated half the members on the advice of the intendant, and the assembly itself was to co-opt the remainder. Secondly, on the plea that the assemblies were untried institutions, they were to be strictly controlled by the intendants. There was in consequence a public outcry that the govern-ment had not conceded any representation or decentralization, and that no economies or reforms would result. The government hesitated, and the *Parlements* pressed home their advantage.

The check to the idea of provincial assemblies rallied public opinion in support of provincial Estates and the Estates-General, traditional institutions approved by the *Parlements*, which now seemed able to dictate to the king. When Brienne presented proposals for fresh taxation, the *Parlements* rejected them with contempt and demanded the calling of the Estates-General. They became so arrogant that in August 1787 Brienne exiled the *Parlement* of Paris to Troyes. Thereafter until May 1788 the *Parlements* bombarded the government with protests and remonstrances, claiming to speak in the name of the nation and using the ideas of the *philosophes* and of Rousseau. 'That man is born free,' the *Parlement* of Brittany asserted, 'that originally men are equal, these are truths that have no need of proof. One of the first needs of society is that individual wills should always yield to the general will.'

Goaded beyond endurance, in May 1788 the government suppressed the power of the *Parlements* to register ordinances and entrusted this power to a new *Cour Plénière*. The *Parlements* had the choice between submission and resistance. Conscious of strong support, they chose to fight; and the resulting furore, often called *la révolte nobiliaire*, might well be more widely termed 'the revolt of the privileged classes'. The Assembly of Clergy remonstrated against the suspension of the *Parlements* and proclaimed the immunity of the clergy from taxation. The dukes and peers of France publicly supported the *Parlements*. The nobility came to the defence of the magistrates, for they saw that their own privileges might be attacked next. Supported by the aristocracy, the magistrates organized riots in the provincial capitals, at Bordeaux, Dijon, Pau, Toulouse. In Brittany the Estates and the *Parlement* opposed the proposed reforms on the ground that they broke the terms of the union of Brittany with France, and the intendant had to flee to Paris. At Grenoble in Dauphiné not only did the citizens riot against the governor but the Estates of Dauphiné, suppressed by Richelieu in 1628, met unbidden and demanded meetings of the Estates-General and the provincial Estates. This was the general programme of the *Parlements*. In Franche-Comté the Estates met for the first time since 1678, in Provence for the first time since 1639.

Faced by such widespread revolt of the privileged classes, the government gave in. On 8 August 1788 the Estates-General was summoned to meet on 1 May 1789, and the *Cour Plénière* was suspended. During the following months of 1788 the new chief minister,

64 'The day of the tiles': street fighting in the Grenoble riots of June–July 1788.

Necker, revoked the edict to set up provincial assemblies and issued a new edict to provide for provincial Estates all over France, with annual meetings, increased powers, and double representation for the third estate. In September 1788 the triumphant *Parlement* of Paris registered the edict summoning the Estates-General; but true to its legalism and its conservatism, it decreed that the Estates should meet 'in accordance with the forms observed in 1614'.

At once there was an outcry from the unprivileged classes, especially those who had prospered in the eighteenth century but who were excluded from higher office by lack of nobility and humiliated by belonging to a lower caste. Such were the thousands of lower civil servants, of lawyers, of physicians and surgeons, of engineers and surveyors, of merchants and bankers – the men who did the organizing of the country but were shut out of positions of power and honour. The claim of the *Parlements* to represent the nation was revealed as false; and two conceptions of what the Estates-General should be were brought into fierce conflict. Suddenly the target of popular hatred in hundreds of pamphlets ceased to be the government and became the

141

65 Louis XVI receiving members of the *noblesse de robe*, soon to fall from their privileged position.

privileged orders. The government was bombarded with petitions for double representation for the third estate and voting by head instead of by order. The leaders of the bourgeoisie and the lower clergy turned against the privileged orders all the weapons of subversion that they had learnt from the *Parlements*. So great became the clamour that in December the royal council considered the question of double representation for the third estate. Necker, whose guiding principle was always to keep his popularity, advised the king to agree, and at a stroke the revolt of the privileged classes was defeated. By this measure the transition from a representative assembly organized by orders to one based on classes was made possible.

When the Estates-General met, it was at once apparent that there was a clear majority in favour of an attack on privilege. Not only did the third estate have double representation, with 661 deputies, but there was a majority for reform in the order of clergy, where 220 out of 326 were members of the unprivileged parish clergy. If only voting by head could be achieved there would be a clear majority for reform, especially as a small group of liberal nobles was sympathetic to it. Among them, the Marquis de Mirabeau dreamt of reform along

66 The deputies leaving for the Estates-General at Versailles, 1789. The third estate, with double representation, is firmly in control, while the nobility and clergy, divided within their ranks, balance precariously.

the lines of the British constitution. This seemed to be brought nearer when, in the early summer of 1789, parties of deputies began to form under the cover of provincial clubs; the Breton club soon became the Jacobin club. When, at the end of June, the Estates-General became the National Assembly, the transition from the society of orders to the society of classes, with decisions taken by majorities, brought the government of France nearer to that of Great Britain. But in the situation of 1789 Mirabeau's conception had no chance of success. Its only hope would have been a strong and understanding king; and Louis XVI was not the man. The fall of the Bastille may have saved the National Assembly from a counter-revolution, but it released forces which no one could foresee or control. These forces were rapidly to produce a social revolution with an appeal that extended throughout Europe. Three of its aims – the unity of the nation, the sovereignty of the people, and the equality in status of its citizens – were to arouse a sympathetic response almost everywhere, sweeping away or transforming almost all the older parliaments of Europe. The year 1789 marks the end of the first great era of parliaments and Estates in Europe.

143

The Chancellors
Seat

V CONCLUSION

After 1789, not only in France but in the countries of Europe overrun by her armies, the monarchies and the old Estates went down together. Their common fate may seem surprising when one recalls the clashes between princes and parliaments in the early history of those institutions. Almost without exception, the assemblies had been born at a time when kings were struggling with the Church and the nobility. Kings at times had formally to admit the right of resistance, as did John of England in 1215, Andrew II of Hungary in 1222, and Philip the Fair of France in 1314. Trade improved at a time when, in many parts of western Europe, the rulers were not strong enough to control the towns which prospered with commerce; and in Germany, Italy, southern France, and Spain the towns formed leagues that either defied their rulers at times or treated on something like equal terms with them. The development of civil and canon law in the twelfth and thirteenth centuries, building on Germanic notions of freedom and community and on economic and social realities, encouraged ideas of the corporate rights of clergy, nobles and towns. Both the climate of opinion and the realities of the situation combined to induce rulers to consult these powerful and increasingly self-conscious groups, especially as the development of the notion of representation in Roman-canonical procedure provided an answer to the problem of how to consult, fruitfully, large groups of persons. The greater nobles and higher clergy might be few enough and important enough to consult personally; but the lesser nobles, lower clergy, and the townsmen were too numerous for discussions with the prince, except through representatives. The resulting assemblies were, at this stage in western culture, necessary to the ruler, both positively to enable him to achieve financial or administrative aims that would otherwise have been impossible, and negatively to avert social explosions in the form of revolts or other forms of defiance.

Nevertheless, in the early days of assemblies those summoned had a fair degree of independence which they were not afraid to use and

67 Elizabeth I in Parliament.

68, 69 In the early days of parliaments, the assembly was idealistically upheld as the guarantee of justice *(left)* and the safeguard against tyranny *(right)*.

which the ruler often found disagreeable. Diets insisted on their right to exercise a real control over the levy of taxation, since it was generally believed that rulers had no right to direct taxation (as distinct from tolls or customs) without the consent of the free tax-payer. The clergy were especially indignant at what they regarded as an infringement of clerical immunities. Parliaments also protested against injustice on the part of the ruler, whether positive injustice in the form of alleged breach of feudal rights, clerical rights or customary rights, or negative injustice in the form of failure to take action to protect what were regarded as natural or customary rights. It was no accident that the presentation of petitions and the hearing of cases was a very early feature in the development of parliaments, some of which, as in Spain, made arrangements for the supervision of justice in their name between the sessions. And as the assemblies changed from being mere occasions into something like regular institutions, they claimed to advise the king in his conduct of affairs or choice of ministers, even occasionally claiming to participate in his deposition if he failed too conspicuously in the exercise of his kingly functions, whether in administration or in war. In an age when the election of kings had not been forgotten, it was common for Estates to claim an important role in the process by which a new king was raised to the throne. They also asserted their right to participate in government during a minority, and to have a voice when a dynasty became extinct or when the succession was disputed. In many areas – notably in Germany – they opposed the cession or partition of the state. The opposition of the more powerful estates in the Diets might break out at any time if the ruler was considered weak or tyrannical or if an unforeseen crisis should occur.

Nevertheless, rulers persevered in calling meetings of Diets; for not only could they be of use, if properly managed, for internal matters such as granting taxes, helping in the administration of justice, or even in preparing legislation, but they might be useful in a prince's dispute with the pope or with a foreign ruler, to show that the prince had the support of the important groups in the stand that he had taken. From the prince's point of view, it was generally more valuable to have an assembly drawn from the whole of his dominions, but in view of the strength of local and particularist sentiment and interests, this was hard to achieve. The king of England could, because of the early strength of the English monarchy, insist on the attendance of nobles, clergy, and deputies from nearly the whole of his realm of England; but this was exceptional, and even he thought it impossible or unwise to insist on representatives from Wales, Cheshire or Durham before the sixteenth century, and quite out of the question to ask for deputies from Ireland or Gascony. In one or two other states (such as Castile or Denmark) the king was strong enough to insist on a common assembly for the whole realm; but a more usual pattern was for the king to have to acquiesce in local or regional Estates as well as encouraging nation-wide assemblies. Law and custom varied from region to region, and the dominant social groups of the different regions wished to have an assembly of their own; then they could be sure that their local views and interests would find clear expression, unhampered by the louder or conflicting voices of other regions.

This explains why in France the provincial Estates were more firmly grounded than the Estates-General; in Germany the *Reichstag* was a late and weak development compared with the *Landtage* of the principalities. Princes who expanded their dominions, like the Habsburgs, Hohenzollerns or Wittelsbachs, found that they had to put up with the continued existence of separate *Landtage* for the different provinces of their domains, with all the variations in policy, structure and relationships that that involved. As for Poland and Hungary, the central administration was never established as firmly as in a country like France, and the force of local sentiment and aristocratic wishes continued to be much stronger. In France provincial assemblies survived, generally speaking, on the periphery of the kingdom, in provinces added late to the direct rule of the king and hence retaining a stronger sense of identity; but in Poland and Hungary local assemblies were universal, their powers were great in local government, and the king had to be wary in dealing with them. And whereas in western Europe the king usually had enough power to insist that the aristocratic voice in the central assembly should be limited to an estate of nobles, in Poland and Hungary not only were the leading nobles present personally in an Upper House, but the lesser nobility were represented in a Lower House, chosen by the local assemblies.

Almost everywhere in Europe the power of local feeling was strong enough to enable the local communities to insist that their deputies must have a limited mandate and must refer back if unexpected demands were made in the central assembly. Here again, as Professor Cam once said, 'England is the square peg that will not fit into the round hole'; before the end of the thirteenth century the monarchy was strong enough to insist that representatives must come to Parliament with full powers, to 'do whatever in the aforesaid matters may be ordained by common counsel; and so that, through default of such authority, the aforesaid business shall by no means remain unfinished'.

By the end of the fifteenth century the balance of social and political forces was changing enough to affect significantly the relationships between princes and parliaments. The shift was not in one direction only, and it was not until the late sixteenth century that most men

70 Strong monarchy in France: Henry IV as Jupiter, enthroned in the clouds.

could begin to see the general direction of the currents. In western Europe, conditions were favourable for the development of strong monarchies in the early sixteenth century. The monarchies of England, France and Spain had all emerged victorious from civil war with over-mighty subjects. Even before the Reformation they had established themselves as the dominant partners in their alliance with the Church, for example in the appointment of bishops, the levy of taxation from the clergy, and the pursuit of heretics. They had succeeded in making the monarchy militarily stronger than any internal force, and though this tempted them into adventures abroad, they were able to keep solvent by a variety of financial expedients, ranging from sale of offices and revival of feudal dues to loans and taxes. They were able to insist on their sole control of foreign policy and even to take a greater initiative in legislation.

71 *(Left)* The king as Grand Master of Calatrava: Spanish monarchs curbed the power of the knights by placing themselves at the head of the knightly orders.

72 *(Right)* Even Henry VIII, who generally got his own way, found it prudent to take Parliament into partnership.

But the Reformation, contrary to what is often thought, tended for a time to make the monarchy more dependent on the co-operation of the estates. The Spanish monarchy found itself increasingly involved in wars against the Protestant powers and the Turks, and in most of its dominions had to appeal to the local parliament – whether in Aragon, Sicily, Naples, or the Netherlands – for increased financial aid. In this matter Castile was a conspicuous exception. In France, the monarchy, which had not summoned a full Estates-General since 1484, had to hold a series of meetings to attempt to deal with religious strife. In England Henry VIII found it expedient to call Parliament into partnership to effect the breach with Rome; it was then discovered

73 A meeting of the *Reichstag* in the sixteenth century, with the Holy Roman Emperor presiding.

that the conflicts abroad and at home aroused by the Reformation necessitated increased reliance on Parliament for the taxation that the prince must have to meet these dangers.

In central and northern Europe the rulers were usually in a weaker position, and for a while were driven by the Reformation into even greater reliance on their Diets. In Scandinavia the *Riksdagar* were used, as in England, to associate the principal social groups (other than the few papalist clergy) with the cause of Reform. In the Protestant states of Germany, the Reformation was carried out by the prince, and the bishops disappeared as an independent force; but through financial necessity most princes had to sell the Church lands quickly and then turn to the *Landtag* for money to protect them from Catholic attack. The *Landtage* used the opportunity to gain fresh privileges and some say in church affairs. Their position became stronger; in the secularized duchy of Prussia they became the real masters of the country. In a number of states where the prince remained Catholic, most of his subjects became Protestant; this was especially the case in Bavaria, Austria, and Bohemia. Here the *Landtage* found for a while a stronger role as the mouthpiece of opposition to the prince, the Jesuits, and the Inquisition; a few of them won victories in this field, as for example in Styria, where in the 1570s the *Landtag* gained full religious liberty from Maximilian II. In Hungary and Poland, too, the Diets became rallying-points for the opposition of Calvinist nobility to Catholic kings.

By the seventeenth century, however, the tide had turned against most of the parliaments of Europe. A few had increased in strength. In England the Parliament defeated the king in civil war and abolished the monarchy; and though this was restored after eleven years, its power in relation to the Parliament was never to be as strong again. In the Netherlands the provincial Estates and the States-General had between them become the rulers of the country in the long struggle against Spain. In Sweden Gustavus Vasa enhanced the power of the *Riksdag* to aid both the unity of the country and the increase of his own power. In Poland the power of the nobility had grown so rapidly with the enserfment of the peasantry and the enfeeblement of the monarchy, especially after 1572, that the Diet and the dietines were by the seventeenth century clearly of more consequence in the government than the king. But the Netherlands could be discounted as a special case; England and Poland were commonly regarded in the latter part of the century as warnings of the evils of over-powerful parliaments; and the balance in Sweden swung in favour of the monarchy as its prestige grew with its lengthening record of dazzling success in international warfare. The brilliant spectacle of Louis XIV seemed to clinch the argument, already put forward with increasing force by many writers, that the way ahead lay with absolute monarchy, whether for the internal peace and law of the realm, or for the prosperity, unity, and power of a kingdom. The power and symbolism of a Sun King would be dimmed or hindered if it had to be shared with a fractious parliament.

Another factor which on the whole worked against the Estates was

74 The Emperor Charles V (right of centre) praying, with members of the royal family and (foreground) Old Testament figures. The Counter-Reformation strengthened the hand of the Catholic monarchies.

the recovery of Catholicism, first in the Counter-Reformation and then in the Thirty Years War. Catholic apologists developed the comparison between the duty of obedience to God and the duty of obedience to a Catholic prince, while the Jesuits and the Inquisition backed the Catholic monarchies, to promote the true faith and to suppress heresies. The defeat of Protestantism in Bavaria and Austria was a defeat for the Estates; the sweeping victory over Protestantism in Bohemia was also a crushing blow for the Estates of that realm, since it was they who had invited the Calvinist Frederick V to reign over them. In the Palatinate the Catholic Maximilian of Bavaria abolished the Estates when he overran the electorate, and the restored Calvinist elector found absolute government more agreeable. For Protestant rulers too could find absolute monarchy attractive, and in Brandenburg the Great Elector's arbitrary levy of the urban excise made it unnecessary to summon any more meetings of the *Landtag*. In Denmark in 1660 the remedy for military disaster seemed to lie in the introduction of absolute monarchy; it would not have appeared an obvious remedy two centuries earlier.

It has often been noted that the age of absolute monarchy was also the age of the disappearance of many Estates. What has less frequently been observed is that many Diets survived. In Poland and Hungary the decay of the towns meant that the Diets were now exclusively dominated by the nobility, which in Poland was able to control both the administration of the realm and the economic and social structure of Polish society. In central, western, and southern Europe the surviving Estates usually became tamed and co-operative, a subordinate element in the machinery of government. In Languedoc the French government looked to the Estates to collect some taxes and see to public works. This it did very efficiently under the guidance of the three archbishops and twenty bishops. At the end of each annual session deputies went from the meeting (always at Montpellier from 1736) to the royal court to present the remonstrances of the Estates, and were received with the grand ceremonial accorded to foreign ambassadors. The Estates employed secretaries, tax-collectors, and other officials, including a permanent agent in Paris. Similar functions were performed (rather less efficiently) by the Estates of Brittany. In the Boulonnais, French Flanders, Béarn, and Burgundy the royal intendants relied for tax collection and public works on committees of Estates. But all these Estates accepted direction from the government on the amounts of taxation and the programmes of works that were required; when, in 1763, the Estates of Brittany refused to finance the construction of the new network of royal roads, the shock was so great that it caused a nation-wide crisis.

A similar use of Estates can be found in Germany and Austria, where committees of Estates performed a variety of functions ranging from the assessment and collection of taxes, and the supervision of public works, especially roads, to the levying of troops and horses for the army. One of the most elaborate of such organizations was to be found in Styria. There the Estates had in the sixteenth century put up vigorous opposition to the Habsburgs on the religious question; by the early eighteenth century it was acting as an important part of the civil service. The Estates office at Graz was bigger than that of the average French intendant. It supervised the military establishment along the Turkish frontier, controlled the medical service of the province, organized the customs and the royal woods and forests; until 1778 it even appointed the province's professors of law. In fact, owing to the accumulation of offices many officials, not only in Styria, were employed both by the Estates and by the prince – sometimes simultaneously. And even in the rare cases where the parliament was dominant in the state, as in England after 1714 or in Sweden between 1720 and 1772, there was an interpenetration of the patronage of Crown and parliament. In contrast to the dualism of the old-style *Ständestaat*, rulers and parliaments were becoming woven together as part of an interlocking governmental and social network.

This process was much assisted by an important development in the societies of western Europe. Though they differed in detail from country to country and even to a certain extent from region to region, all shared the characteristic that from the later seventeenth century they were becoming more aristocratic. There was a strengthening of the notion that there were some orders of men whose function it was to fill positions of authority in Church and state, and there was also a strengthening of the tendency towards the inheritance of this right in a governing class, either by law or in fact. These trends were so vigorous that even where, as in France, the monarchy had tried in the late seventeenth century to choose its servants by talent rather than by rank, in the early eighteenth century the aristocracy captured the machinery of state created by Louis XIV and his ministers. Everywhere there was a tendency for greater store to be set on noble status,

75 A representative addressing the Council of Berne, which was a stiff and aristocratic gathering as early as 1584.

and for the governing classes to close ranks. For example, the magistrates of the *Parlements* of France were in 1600 despised by the nobility, but by the reign of Louis XV no one doubted that they were nobles. They were educated in the same schools as the nobility of the sword. They dressed in the same manner, drove about in carriages, flocked to the theatre, fought duels, attended salons, owned sumptuous mansions, bought Bohemian crystal and Sèvres china, tapestries, and fine pictures. They married into noble families as old as the Montmorencys and the La Rochefoucaulds, and were presented at court. The Dutch ruling class of regent burghers were despised by the Spaniards of the reign of Philip II as mere traders; by the middle of the eighteenth century their descendants were regarded as patricians, to be treated as nobles and received at foreign courts as such. In the city of Berne no one was admitted to the citizenship between 1651 and 1790, so that the citizenship became purely hereditary. Examples might be multiplied.

The result was that, outside Great Britain, the membership of Diets or parliaments came to be dominated by aristocratic sentiments and values. In many parts of Europe the towns had suffered a sharp economic decline, and their representation in the Diets had either disappeared, as in Hungary or Poland, or it had itself become aristo-

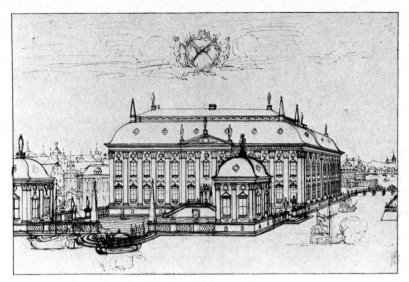

76 The *Riddarhus*, House of Nobles in the Swedish *Riksdag*.

cratic, as in Spain or Languedoc. Indeed the Estates of Languedoc, meeting annually until they were swept away by the Revolution, are a striking example of this dominance of aristocratic values. There the third estate had double representation and voting was by head, the two points which were to have such revolutionary consequences in the National Assembly when they were generally conceded in 1789. But in Languedoc the Estates remained a peaceful and integral part of the established order until 1789, for the representatives of the third estate, the *syndics* of the towns, regarded themselves as lesser nobility, and, provided their privileges and dignity were respected, they were perfectly prepared to accept the lead of the archbishops and bishops (themselves chosen from the higher nobility) and the greater lay nobles. In Sweden the *Riksdag* included the estates of peasants and burghers; but the nobles dominated the kingdom, especially during the Age of Liberty, from 1720 to 1772. The Secret Committee of the *Riksdag* was composed of fifty nobles, twenty-five churchmen, and twenty-five burghers. The government was controlled by a council of nobles, of whom the king was only the chairman. The nobles claimed the exclusive right to high office; entry to the rank of noble other than by birth was rare, and a law of 1762 decreed that no new families could enter the *Riddarhus*, the House of Nobles in the *Riksdag*.

157·

77 Gustavus III opening the *Riksdag* in the Hall of State, Stockholm, in 1789.

This growing integration of the parliaments of Europe with the established order did not guarantee an absence of clashes with governments. In the last decades of the old régime the reforming emperor Joseph II found himself in conflict with the Estates in Hungary and Bohemia and the Austrian Netherlands, so much so that when he died in 1790 a revolution had broken out in Belgium. He wanted (as he saw it) rational social change; the alarmed assemblies of provincial Estates took their stand on constitutional liberties. Joseph II had seen Belgium as a confused and torpid museum of late medieval privileges, and thought that it would be a service to humanity as well as to efficiency to modernize it. To his astonishment he was confronted by apparently universal opposition. At the close of 1788 the Estates of Brabant and Hainault refused to grant any taxes to the emperor; Joseph II thereupon declared the constitutional charter of Brabant, the Joyous Entry of 1356, to be abrogated.

This was the spark that started a revolution, early in 1789, before the Estates-General had met in France. In Brussels a brewer painted the door of his house with the colours of Brabant – red, yellow, black;

it was the first tricolour. Each province declared its independence, and Austrian resistance collapsed, largely because the Austrians were taken by surprise and had so few troops available, since they were fighting the Turks. But as soon as independence seemed to have been gained so easily, divergences appeared between the opponents of the Austrians. The Estates of Brabant, officially suppressed, met and invited the Estates of other provinces to send delegates to a conference. When this conference met, it proclaimed itself to be the Estates-General of the (Belgian) Netherlands. Its Act of Union followed the American Articles of Confederation; but its aim was entirely conservative, to keep all the local assemblies, laws, and customs as they were before Joseph II began his reforms. But these assemblies represented the abbots and higher clergy, the nobles, and the hereditary councillors of the towns; and many middle-class people – merchants, shopkeepers, printers, industrialists, lawyers, surgeons, physicians, and a few parish priests – inspired by the American and French revolutions and the writings of a Brussels lawyer, J.F. Vonck, protested against the perpetuation of a constitution which excluded them from both political power and social equality. They called themselves Democrats – probably the first party in Europe to do so – and described their opponents as Aristocrats.

The Democrats at this stage were very moderate, but the Estates party feared that they were the spearhead of revolution. A reign of terror began, fostered especially by the monastic clergy, and the supporters of Vonck were arrested, silenced, driven into exile. In France the exiles got in touch with the agents of the Emperor Leopold II, who, taking advantage of these deep dissensions in Belgium, re-established Austrian rule in December 1790. The exiles poured back again, now much more radical than they had been, after contact with the stirring events in France. The Austrian government began to be afraid of them, and government and aristocratic estates began to draw together in common fear of the French Revolution. Then, in November 1792, the French republican army poured into the Austrian Netherlands and brought the old régime there to an abrupt end.

The course of the revolution in Belgium brings out two important points about the final years of the old Estates in Europe. First, the widespread discontent with the existing order was not confined to France; it was not initiated by the French Revolution, though of course the success of the revolution at home and its military victories in Europe greatly encouraged the forces of change. Apart from the American Revolution, there had already been opposition to the established order before 1789 in the United Provinces and in Switzerland, in England and in Ireland; and though the influence of the French Revolution was felt in the upheavals in Belgium and in Poland, the ferment had already begun there before events in France took a radical turn in 1791. Many contemporaries perceived at an early stage that the crisis was not merely French but international. Peter Ochs, a member of one of the ruling families in Basle who gradually swung over to the revolutionary side, remarked in 1792: 'The revolutions of America, France, and Poland obviously belong in a chain of events that will regenerate the world.' Secondly, the aristocratic parliaments might be at odds with the princes, as the regent burghers in the Netherlands were with William V, or the Estates in Belgium with the Austrian monarchy; but when they were confronted with men who wanted to change the foundations of government, to break down existing privileges, with the opportunities they gave of office, wealth and social exclusiveness, and to replace them by elected parliaments, chosen without regard to orders or privileges, the estates realized that they belonged to the same world of ideas as the old monarchies.

The rulers discovered that they felt the same. In 1785, at the height of the agitation of the Patriots in the Netherlands, the young G. K. van Hogendorp urged William V to put himself at the head of the Patriots against the urban regent oligarchs. In 1814 van Hogendorp was to be hailed as a national hero for his role in restoring the House of Orange. But times had changed by then; in 1814 *Stadhouder* William VI, by then King William I of the Netherlands, was to be a national monarch, with a relatively liberal constitution. In 1785 his father, *Stadhouder* William V, could not disown the privileged classes, even if for nearly two hundred years they had been a recurring source of harassment of his family. He could not ally himself with men who contravened all the accepted ideas of his world about those who had a right to share in the government and those who had not. For similar reasons he refused in 1790 an appeal from the Belgian rebels to help them, and an offer to make his second son their hereditary *Stadhouder*. More striking still, the Emperor Leopold II, one of the most reasonable men ever to rule in Europe and willing to go to great lengths to conciliate reformers, was forced by 1792 through fear of the French Revolution into a position of supporting aristocratic estates and privileged classes. When the Revolution came to the different countries of western and central Europe, monarchy and estates went down together.

In only one country of Europe did the old parliament come through this period unscathed – Great Britain. For all the resemblances of British society in the eighteenth century in manners and morals to that of France, there was in the British system of society and government a greater unity and openness that was eventually to make possible reform instead of revolution. As Defoe had expressed it:

> *Fate has but little Distinction set*
> *Betwixt the Counter and the Coronet.*

In England the army counted for less than it did in France, Spain, Prussia, Austria, or Russia; and in England the soldier had less and the merchant more prestige than their counterparts in these countries. There was in eighteenth-century England an absence of legal privilege, a closer connection between the gentry and the businessmen, an equality before the law, a national unity, a freedom from irksome economic restrictions, a sensitivity of the government to commercial interests and business methods, which were making English society the most firmly grounded and the most progressive in Europe. And for all the deference in England to nobility and rank, it was plain to everyone that the most decisive element in government was already the House of Commons, to which some at least of the members were actually elected by voters who included relatively humble folk. Though there was to be severe controversy in the process, it was possible for Britain to move without revolution into the world of nineteenth-century liberalism.

In trying to explain how events and movements occur, it is only too easy for the historian to justify success, and to imply, if not to say, that what actually came to be deserved to be. It is easy to see the defects of the old parliaments from the standpoint of the late twentieth century. By the eighteenth century, in most countries where they still functioned, they had hardened into bastions of unthinking conservatism, intent on defending privileges that had lost their original justification, obstructing all attempts at reforms that might have ameliorated or solved the political and social problems of the day. Yet it is possible that their catastrophic abolition was not inevitable. We must remember, for example, that the *Riksdag* of Sweden continued in its old form of four estates until 1866, and was then transformed, quite peacefully, into a modern parliament. As one distinguished historian of the French Revolution has said: 'The changes in French society and the revolution in ideas were perhaps bound to find their reflection in political and institutional developments sooner or later; but this is not equivalent to saying that the French Revolution was inevitable. What form the impending social and political changes were to take, and when they were to come about and how, were matters to be decided by circumstance.' (A. Cobban)

There is also a more positive aspect of the old estates which, because it is quite out of fashion, is perhaps worthy of some attention. It is arguable that the replacement of the old assemblies of estates by modern-style parliaments was not all pure gain. It is not only that a liberal parliament could, as in France's July Monarchy, be dominated by rich men pursuing *laissez-faire* policies and apparently indifferent to the sufferings of the urban masses; there were also deeper dangers.

78 *(Above)* The House of Commons in 1793: alone among European assemblies, the British Parliament survived the eighteenth century without a change of form.

79 *(Below)* Candidates canvassing support prior to the Westminster election of 1796.

It was at that time that Comte Alexis de Tocqueville, by no means a defender of the old régime, saw, with almost startling prescience, the ultimate danger of the democratic urge as likely to be, not weakness and confusion, but uniformity and despotism. He realized that the effect of the French Revolution had been not to weaken government but to strengthen it, by its improvement in the efficiency of administration, its power to harness national resources to public ends, its undermining of regional and local customs and loyalties. He perceived that the power of government was increased by every fresh invention of transport, of weapons, of communications, of administrative techniques. He understood that the drive towards equality might be at the expense of liberty and variety, that the urge to destroy every vestige of privilege might leave the isolated individual undefended by any non-state group or institution, at the mercy of a state mighty enough to command, in the name of the people, not only the obedience of his body but, by its power of controlling public opinion, the subjection of his mind.

If the state is not all-powerful and all-pervading in the countries of western Europe or North America, it is unlikely that this is due primarily to written constitutional guarantees or declarations of the rights of man; the Weimar constitution availed nothing when the Nazis took control. It is probably more fundamental that, in these countries of western Europe and North America, there are still important groupings of power independent of the state, drawing their authority, their basic rights, and their vitality from other sources, however much they may co-operate with the government. It is significant that in France, where in the Revolution the doctrine of the state one and indivisible was proclaimed, with the abolition of all independent corporations and traditional institutions, there should now be a movement to give back some autonomy to the historic regions, so that the feelings of freedom and variety may be strengthened. By the eighteenth century the activities of most of the old Estates were vitiated by their clinging to outworn privileges, by a narrowing 'class consciousness', and by obstructive inherited rights. But they did sense that the power of the ruler would be irresistible unless there were independent groups with power. There may be more connection between the spirit of the old rallying-cries of 'the rights of the Estates' or 'the customs of the provinces', and the vitality of parliamentary government, than it is now popular to admit.

SELECT BIBLIOGRAPHY

Note on manuscripts in Paris and Barcelona

Paris

For the Estates-General there is no great series comparable to the wealth of records available for the British or Hispanic parliaments. In the Archives Nationales there are a number of records in boxes K674 to K679 relating to meetings of the Estates-General from 1484 to 1789. It was to one of these (K676, No. 9, the memoir of Cardinal Dubois to the Regent Orléans, expressing shock and horror at this idea of convoking the Estates-General) that reference was made above (Chapter III, page 69).

A large proportion of what has survived is concerned with the ferment of the years from 1787 onwards. Boxes K677 and K678 are concerned with the assemblies of notables in 1787 and 1788, and Box K679 deals with the proceedings of the Estates-General of 1789 and the National Assembly. Again, boxes K680 to K692 are concerned with meetings of provincial Estates and provincial assemblies from 1439 to 1789; but the great bulk of the records deals with the provincial assemblies of 1787 and the provincial elections for the Estates-General of 1789.

It is perhaps natural that for earlier periods, when the Estates-General was less valued, many of the documents slipped out of official custody, and, if they survived at all, sometimes found their way eventually into the Bibliothèque Nationale. Such manuscripts may be found in MS. FR. 7517–23, 10867–83, 16248–58, 16262–66. It is significant that a larger proportion than in the records of the British Parliament is concerned with questions of procedure and ceremonial.

Barcelona

In contrast to the Estates-General of France, the *Cortes* of Aragon has left behind a great mass of material. It is well described in the *Guia abreviada* of the Archivo de la Corona de Aragón. Unfortunately the only part of the records which appears to be well arranged is the first section, which includes documents of the proceedings and acts of the *Cortes*, many of which were printed in *Cortes de los Antiquos Reinos de Aragón y de Valencia* (1896–   ). Until the documents in the other classes are adequately sorted and calendared it will not be possible for scholars to make adequate use of them. A useful collection of documents is that compiled by Carlos Riba y Garcia in his book *El Consejo supremo de Aragón en el reinado de Felipe II* (1915). Besides a useful survey of the *Cortes* of Aragon in the introduction, pp. xxviii–xxxiii, it includes documents from Add. MSS. 28382 and 28383 in the British Museum. These are records of the Council of Aragon in the years 1587 to 1589. There is in the British Museum a volume, Add. MS. 28434, of proceedings of the *Cortes* of Castile between 1518 and 1583, copied from papers at Simancas.

General Works

Most of the important contributions before 1955 are listed in *Recent Works on the Origins and Development of Representative Assemblies*, ed. H. M. Cam, A. Marongiu, and G. Stökl (Florence, 1955), reprinted from *Relazioni de X Congresso Internazionale di Scienze Storiche*. Still fundamental, even if criticized, are the contributions of Otto Hintze, notably 'Typologie der ständischen Verfassungen des Abendlandes' and 'Weltgeschichtliche Bedingungen der Repräsentativ-verfassung', in *Historische Zeitschrift*, Vol. 141 (1929) pp. 229–47 and Vol. 143 (1931) pp. 1–47; these essays have been reprinted in O. Hintze's *Staat und Verfassung* (1962). Also still of value are E. Lousse, *La Société d'Ancien Régime* (1943); O. Brunner, *Land und Herrschaft* (1942); and D. Gerhard, 'Regionalismus und Ständisches Wesen', in *Historische Zeitschrift* Vol. 174 (1952), pp. 307–37. For the English-speaking reader the article by R. B. Lord, 'The Parliaments of the Middle Ages and the Early Modern Period', in *Catholic Historical Review*, Vol. 16 (1930), pp. 125–44 is a useful introduction, and D. Gerhard, 'Assemblies of Estates and the Corporate Order', in *Liber Memorialis Georges de Lagarde* (1970), pp. 283–308, though very general in treatment, is by an historian of great experience in this field.

Useful contributions on the idea of representative assemblies outside western Christendom include E. Szlechter's 'Les Assemblées en Mésopotamie Ancienne', in *Liber Memorialis Georges de Lagarde* (1970), pp. 1–21; C. P. Kyrris, 'Representative Assemblies and Taxation in the Byzantine Empire between 1204 and 1341' in *Studies presented to the International Commission for the History of Representative and Parliamentary Institutions* (hereafter referred to as *International Commission Studies*), Vol. 31 (1966), pp. 43–54; V. Al. Georgesco, 'Types et Formes d'Assemblées d'Etats en droit féodal romain', in *Liber Memorialis Georges de Lagarde* (1970), pp. 113–31; G. I. Bratianu, 'Les Assemblées d'Etats dans les principautés roumaines', in *International Commission Studies*, Vol. 11 (1952), pp. 187–252; G. I. Bratianu, 'Les assemblées d'états en Europe orientale au moyen âge et l'influence du régime politique byzantin', in *Actes du VIe Congrès inter-*

national d'Etudes Byzantines, Tome I (Paris 1950), pp. 35–56; G. Stojcević, 'Gouvernés et gouvernants dans la Serbie médiévale', in *Recueils de la Société Jean Bodin pour l'histoire comparative des institutions*, Vol. 25 (1965), pp. 309–37. (Volumes 22 to 27 of the *Recueils* are concerned with the relationships between those who are governed and those who govern. Hereafter these volumes will be referred to as *Recueils Société Jean Bodin*.)

On the much-discussed topic of the *Zemski Sobor*, J. L. H. Keep reviewed the present state of the question in his essay 'The Decline of the Zemsky Sobor' in *Slavonic and East European Review*, Vol. 36 (1957–58), pp. 100–22. G. Stökl, in the essay previously cited (*Recent Work*, etc.) emphasizes the differences between assemblies in Greek and Latin Christendom; a Marxist interpretation will be found in L. Tcherepnine, 'Le rôle des Zemski Sobory en Russie lors de la guerre des paysans au début du XVIIᵉ siècle', in *Album Helen Cam*, Vol. 1 (1960), pp. 249–66. The inquirer should still read V. O. Klyuchevsky's *History of Russia*, Vol. 3 (1913); though much criticized and opposed, Klyuchevsky's description of the rise and decline of the *Zemski Sobor* remains a very impressive analysis of the phenomenon. N. V. Riasanovsky, *A History of Russia* (1963) has an interesting discussion of the rival theories of the *Zemski Sobor* (pp. 210–12). Some stimulating descriptions of other forms of government in other civilizations will be found in *Recueils Société Jean Bodin*, Vol. 22, *Gouvernés et Gouvernants, Civilisations Archaïques, Islamiques et Orientales*.

The Development of Estates in Europe

General

The reader may well begin with A. Marongiu, *Medieval Parliaments, a Comparative Study* (revised 1962, English trans. 1968), which discusses the general problems before coming to particular countries. In the latter section it is strongest, as might be expected, on the Italian parliaments. Useful essays on general questions are: W. Mohr: 'Die Auswirkung des Gewaltenstreites im Hochmittelalter auf die Entwicklung von Repräsentationsideen', *Liber Memorialis Georges de Lagarde* (1970), pp. 23–55; E. Lousse, 'Assemblées représentatives et taxation', *International Commission Studies*, Vol. 31 (1966), pp. 19–32; A. Marongiu, 'Principe fondamental de la démocratie et du consentement au XIVᵉ siècle', and B. Lyon, 'Medieval Constitutionalism: a Balance of Power', in *Album Helen Cam*, Vol. 2 (1961), pp. 101–15, 155–83; K. Koranyi, 'Zum Ursprung des Anteils der Städte an der ständischen Versammlungen und Parlamenten im Mittelalter', *Album Helen Cam*, Vol. 1 (1960), pp. 37–53; G. de Lagarde, 'La structure politique et sociale de l'Europe au XIVᵉ siècle', in A. Coville (ed.), *L'organ-*

isation corporative du moyen âge à la fin de l'ancien régime (1939), pp. 91–118; G. de Lagarde, 'Individualisme et corporatisme au moyen âge', and E. Lousse, 'La formation des ordres dans la société médiévale', in A. Coville (ed.), *L'organisation corporative du moyen âge à la fin de l'ancien régime* (1937), pp. 1–60, 61–90; G. Post, 'Plena Potestas and Consent in Medieval Assemblies – a study in Romano-Canonical procedure and the rise of representation', *Traditio*, I (1943), pp. 355–408; G. I. Langmuir, 'Politics and Parliaments in the early thirteenth century', *Etudes sur l'Histoire des Assemblées d'états* (Aix-en-Provence, 1964), pp. 47–62; M. Bloch, *La société féodale* (1940); W. Ullmann, *Principles of Government and Politics in the Middle Ages* (1961); E. Lousse, 'Gouvernés et Gouvernants en Europe occidentale durant le bas moyen âge et les temps modernes', in *Recueils Société Jean Bodin*, Vol. 24 (1966), pp. 7–48.

A useful introduction to the sixteenth-century background is *Europe in the Sixteenth Century*, by H. G. Koenigsberger and G. L. Mosse (1968), and valuable commentaries and documents for the study of parliamentary institutions in Spain, Sicily, France, the Low Countries and England are provided in *Representative Government in Western Europe in the Sixteenth Century* (1968), by G. Griffiths. Information on some parliaments in the early part of this period (Piedmont, Sicily, and the Netherlands), together with a discussion of the powers of deputies in sixteenth-century assemblies, is given in *Estates and Revolutions: Essays in Early Modern European History* by H. G. Koenigsberger (1971), and there are discussions of constitutional development and political thought in sixteenth-century Europe by G. R. Elton and R. R. Betts in Volume 2 of the *New Cambridge Modern History* (1958), Chapters 14 and 15.

The seventeenth and eighteenth centuries are attractively surveyed in E. N. Williams' *The Ancien Régime in Europe: Government and Society in the Major States, 1648–1789* (1970), which deals with the Netherlands, Spain, France, Russia, Prussia, Austria, and Britain, with good bibliographies. E. Lousse's essay, in *Recueils Société Jean Bodin*, Vol. 24 (1966), pp. 7–48, already mentioned, is also useful for this period, as well as two essays in the *New Cambridge Modern History*, Vol. 7, by J. O. Lindsay – Chapter 3, 'The Social Classes and the Foundations of the States', and Chapter 7, 'Monarchy and Administration'. For those who can read German, there are three stimulating general essays – by Dietrich Gerhard, Günter Birtsch, and Gerhard Oestreich – in the volume edited by Dietrich Gerhard, entitled *Ständische Vertretungen in Europa im 17. und 18. Jahrhundert* (1969). R. R. Palmer, *The Age of Democratic Revolution* (1959, 2nd edn. 1964) is especially useful for the generation 1760–1789 in both Europe and America, and the clash of ideas at the time of the American, Belgian and French Revolutions, discussed by Palmer, is set in a wider context by Bertrand de Jouvenal in his book *Du Pouvoir* (1945), translated by J. F. Huntingdon in 1948 as *Power*.

A brief but useful essay by Caroline Robbins discusses 'Why the English Parliament survived the Age of Absolutism. Some Explanations offered by Writers of the 17th and 18th centuries' (*International Commission Studies*, Vol. 18 (1958), pp. 199–213).

Particular countries and states

THE HISPANIC PENINSULA

Much has been written on the well-developed *Cortes* of the Spanish kingdoms; but the best general introduction for the English-speaking reader for the medieval period is still R. B. Merriman, 'The Cortes of the Spanish kingdoms in the Later Middle Ages', *American Historical Review*, Vol. 16 (1910–11), pp. 476–95. The first two volumes of R. Altamira's classic *Historia de España* (4 vols., 1900–10) are also valuable as an introduction. D. Ramos gives a useful survey of more recent work in his *Historia de las Cortes tradicionales de España* (1944). For the *Cortes* of Castile the Real Academia de la Historia published between 1861 and 1903 in five volumes the proceedings of the *Cortes* of Leon and Castile from the origins to 1559, and in 1883 and 1884 printed an introduction in two volumes by Don Manuel Colmeiro; this introduction is still the best history of the Castilian *Cortes*. Less has been done for the *Cortes* of the kingdoms of Aragon, Catalonia and Valencia, in spite of their fame. In 1667 the *Diputacion Permanente del Reyno* published the *Fueros y Observancias del Reyno de Aragón* in two volumes, and from 1847 to 1851 *Procesos de las Antiguas Cortes y Parlamentos de Cataluña, Aragón y Valencia* were published in P. de Bofarull's *Coleccion de Documentos inéditos del Archivo General de la Corona de Aragón* (8 volumes, 1847–51); but there is no good recent study of any of these *Cortes*. The *Historia de la Legislacion y Recitaciones del Derecho Civil de España* (9 vols., 1861–76) is very thorough; and valuable material on the various *Cortes* will be found in *Cortes Catalanas*, by J. Coroleu and R. Pella (1876), Vincente de la Fuente's *Estudios Críticos sobre la Historia y el Derecho de Aragón* (1885), and M. Danvila y Collado's *Estudios Críticos acerca de las Cortes y Parlamentos de Valencia* (1906). The *Cortes* of these eastern realms attracted much attention from seventeenth-century writers; among these Geronimo de Martel's *Forma de celebrar Cortes en Aragón* and Geronimo Blancas' *Modo de proceder en Cortes de Aragón* (both 1641) are still of especial value to the modern reader.

For the later history of the Spanish *Cortes* a useful general introduction will be found in J. Beneyto's essay 'Les Cortes d'Espagne du XVIe au XIXe siècles' in *Recueils Société Jean Bodin*, Vol. 24 (1966), pp. 461–81. In addition to the bibliography there given (pp. 479–81), see J. Lynch, *Spain under the Habsburgs* (2 vols., 1964, 1969). For the difficulties in the way of a reformer in eighteenth-century Spain, see V. Rodriguez Casado, *La Politica y los politicos en el reinado de Carlos III* (1962). P. Vilar, *Spain, A Brief History* (1967) is also useful.

For Portugal the best introduction is H. L. Livermore's *History of Portugal* (1947). Fuller information is available in H. de Gama Barros's *História da administração pública em Portugal nos séculos XII a XV* (1885–1922, 4 vols., revised by T. de Sousa Suarez, 1945————). The acts of the *Cortes* are still unprinted but J. Leitão has published a list, *Cortes do Reino de Portugal: Inventario da documentação existente* (1940).

FRANCE

Etats-Généraux
The best introduction is now probably C. Soule, *Les Etats Généraux de France* (1968), which may be supplemented by consultation of F. Lot and R. Fawtier, *Histoire des institutions françaises au moyen âge, Tome II – Institutions royales* (1958) and F. Olivier-Martin, *Histoire du droit français des origines à la Révolution* (1948). Of the large bulk of writings on the Estates-General the following are probably the most useful for the general reader: H. Hervieu, *Recherche sur les premiers Etats généraux et les assemblées représentatives pendant la première moitié du quatorzième siècle* (1879); G. Picot, *Histoire des Etats Généraux* (2nd edn., 1888, 6 vols.); G. Picot and P. Guerin, *Documents relatifs aux Etats généraux et assemblées réunis sous Philippe le Bel* (Paris, 1901); L. Balas, *Une tentative de gouvernement représentatif au XIVᵉ siècle. Les Etats généraux de 1356–1358* (1928); J. Cadart, *Le régime electoral des Etats généraux de 1789 et ses origines (1302–1614)*; J. Garillot, *Les Etats généraux de 1439* (1947); J. Masselin, *Journal des Etats généraux de France tenus à Tours en 1484 sous le règne de Charles VIII* (1835). See also A. R. Myers, 'The English Parliament and the French Estates-General in the Middle Ages', *Album Helen Cam*, Vol. 2 (1961), pp. 139–53. For the later period see R. Doucet, *Les Institutions de la France au XVIᵉ siècle*, Vol. I (1948), A. D. Lublinskaja, 'Les Etats Généraux de 1614–15 en France' and Fr. Gallouedec-Genuys, 'Fénélon et les Etats', in *Album Helen Cam*, Vol. 1 (1960), pp. 229–46, 277–90, and A. D. Lublinskaja, 'Les Assemblées des Notables de 1617 et de 1626', *International Commission Studies*, Vol. 31 (1966), pp. 163–78.

Provincial Estates
A book that links the history of the Estates-General and that of provincial Estates is J. R. Major's *Representative Institutions in Renaissance France, 1422–1559* (1960). Volume 24 of the *Recueils Société Jean Bodin*, pp. 181–

233, 235–97, has two illuminating articles on 'Gouvernés et Gouvernants en France', the first by Fr. Dumont and P. C. Timbal on the Middle Ages and the sixteenth century, the second by R. Mousnier on the seventeenth and eighteenth centuries. Three useful articles on the general development of the provincial Estates are: G. Dupont-Ferrier, 'De quelques problèmes relatifs aux états provinciaux' (*Journal des Savants*, 1928, pp. 315–57); H. Prentout, 'Les états provinciaux en France' (*Bulletin of the International Committee of Historical Sciences*, 1929, I, 632–47); and Chapter 15 of Doucet, *op. cit.* Ten essays on the provincial Estates in relation to taxation are collected in *Etudes sur l'histoire des assemblées d'états* (Aix-en-Provence, 1964), ed. Fr. Dumont.

For the history of one of the most important assemblies, that of Languedoc, see P. Dognon, *Les institutions politiques et administratives du pays de Languedoc du XIIIᵉ siècle aux guerres de religion* (1896); H. Gilles, *Les états de Languedoc au XVᵉ siècle* (1965); E. Appolis's essays in A. Coville (ed.), *L'organisation corporative du moyen âge à la fin de l'ancien régime* (1937), pp. 129–48, and *Album Helen Cam*, Vol. 1 (1960), pp. 219–48. For the almost equally powerful Estates of Brittany see E. Durtelle de Saint-Sauveur, *Histoire de Bretagne* (2 vols., 1935). For the Estates of Burgundy consult J. Billioud, *Les états de Bourgogne aux XIVᵉ et XVᵉ siècles* (1922) and J. Richard, 'Les états bourguignons' in Vol. 24 of the *Recueils Société Jean Bodin*, pp. 299–324. Of other studies of provincial estates the following are of particular value: H. Prentout, *Les états provinciaux de Normandie* (1925); A. Dussert, *Les états de Dauphiné, 1457–1559* (1923); L. Cadier, *Les états de Béarn depuis leurs origines jusqu'au commencement du XVIᵉ siècle* (1888); A. Thomas, *Les états provinciaux de la France centrale sous Charles VII* (1879).

From the immense literature on the events leading to the summoning of the Estates-General of 1789, one may pick out P. Renouvin's *Les assemblées provinciales de 1787* (1921); and for an attempt to oppose the concept of the aristocratic reaction of the eighteenth century, see W. Doyle, 'Was there an Aristocratic Reaction in Pre-Revolutionary France?' *Past and Present*, No. 57 (November 1972), pp. 97–122. Useful background information may be obtained from: A. B. Cobban, *A History of Modern France*, Vol. 1, (1957); C. B. A. Behrens, *The Ancien Régime* (1967); P. Goubert, *The Ancien Régime* (1973); H. Méthivier, *L'Ancien Régime* (1961).

GERMANY AND AUSTRIA

Probably the most useful general works for the English-speaking reader are G. Barraclough, *The Origins of Modern Germany*, (2nd edn., 1949) and F. L. Carsten, *Princes and Parliaments in Germany from the 15th to the 18th century* (1959). Professor Carsten discusses specifically the development of *Landtage* in Württemberg, Hesse, Saxony, the Palatinate, and Bavaria, and supplies valuable bibliographies. He deals with the Estates of Brandenburg-Prussia in his book *The Origins of Prussia* (1954). Works in German that are especially useful are K. Spangenberg, *Vom Lehnstaat zum Ständestaat* (1912); F. Hartung, *Deutsche Verfassungsgeschichte vom 15. Jahrhundert bis zur Gegenwart* (5th edn., 1950); H. Helbig, 'Ständische Einungsversuche in den mitteldeutschen Territorien am Ausgang des Mittelalters', *Album Helen Cam*, Vol. 2 (1961), pp. 185–209; and H. Helbig, 'Königtum und Ständeversammlungen in Deutschland am Ende des Mittelalters' in *Ancien Pays et assemblées d'Etats*, 24 (1962), pp. 63–92. A useful discussion in French is that by R. Folz, 'Les assemblées d'états dans les principautés allemandes (fin XIIIe–début XVIe siècle)', in *Recueils Société Jean Bodin*, Vol. 25 (1965), pp. 163–91. For the later period see the essays in the same volume by Gerhard Buchda, 'Reichstände und Landstände in Deutschland im 16. und 17. Jahrhundert' (pp. 193–226), and by F.L. Carsten, 'The German Estates in the 18th century' (pp. 227–38). Professor Carsten also has stimulating essays in the *New Cambridge Modern History of Europe*, Vol. 5, Chapter 18, 'The Empire after the Thirty Years War', and Chapter 23, 'The Rise of Brandenburg'. Also valuable are the eight essays on Estates in various principalities and regions of Germany, printed in *Ständische Vertretungen in Europa im 17. und 18. Jahrhundert*, ed. G. Gerhard (1969), and the articles by H. Stradal, 'Stände und Steuern in Österreich', *International Commission Studies*, Vol. 31 (1966), pp. 131–62, and R. Freiin von Oer, 'Estates and Diets in Ecclesiastical Principalities of the Holy Roman Empire (18th Century)', *Liber Memorialis Georges de Lagarde*, ed. A. Marongiu, pp. 259–81. The government of the Tyrol and its *Landtag* were discussed by Nikolaus Grass, 'Aus der Geschichte der Landstände Tirols', published in *Album Helen Cam*, Vol. 2 (1961), pp. 297–324.

THE NETHERLANDS

The Netherlands and Burgundy before the division in 1586
Good bibliographies will be found in the history of Burgundy under the Valois dukes, written by Professor R. Vaughan – *Philip the Bold* (1962), *John the Fearless* (1966), *Philip the Good* (1970), and *Charles the Bold* (1973). Professor J. Dhondt has co-operated with J. Cuvelier and R. Daehaerd in the production since 1948 by the Académie Royale de Belgique of the first volumes of the *Actes des états généraux des anciens Pays Bas*. The principal transactions of the States-General during the brief period of the united Netherlands north and south, under self-government, were edited by M. Gachard, *Actes des Etats-Généraux des Pays Bas, 1576–85* (2 vols., 1861). H. G. Koenigsberger has a useful essay on 'The States General of the Netherlands before the Revolt', in *International Commission Studies*, Vol. 18 (1958), pp. 141–58.

The Southern Netherlands

Thanks especially to the inspiration of Professor Emile Lousse and the impressive list of publications since 1950 of the Section Belge de la Commission Internationale pour l'Histoire des Assemblées d'Etats, more is available in print on the early history of the provincial Estates of what became the Southern Netherlands or Belgium than for any other country of that size. Volume 35 of the Section's series of *Anciens Pays et Assemblées d'Etats (Standen en Landen)* was published in *Recueils Société Jean Bodin* in 1966 as Vol. 24 (1966). Prefaced by a valuable 'Rapport général sur l'Europe Occidentale durant le bas moyen âge et les temps modernes' by E. Lousse (pp. 7–48), this volume contains an essay on 'Les assemblées d'Etats en Belgique avant 1795' (pp. 325–400) by Professor J. Dhondt. A history of the representative assemblies of the Southern Netherlands (including those of its provinces), is given in T. Juste's *Histoire des Etats Généraux des Pays Bas (1465–1790)* (2 vols., 1864). A valuable collection of essays on the development of estates in Brabant, Flanders, Hainault, Liège, Luxembourg, Limbourg, Malines, Namur, Stavelot-Malmédy, Tournai, and Aarschot, has been published in the *Standen en Landen* under the title *Cinq cents ans de vie parlementaire en Belgique (1464–1964)*, in 1965 as Vol. 33 of that series.

The United Netherlands

A useful introduction and bibliography will be found in George Edmundson's *History of Holland* (1922), and fuller discussions in S. J. Fockema Andreae's *De Nederlandse Staat onder de Republiek* (1969) and his *500 Jaren Staten-Generaal in de Nederlanden* (1964). Also valuable is J. Gilissen, 'Les états-généraux en Belgique et aux pays-bas sous l'ancient régime' in the previously mentioned *Recueils Société Jean Bodin*, Vol. 24 (1966), pp. 401–37. There are interesting essays by H. H. Rowen, 'John de Witt: the makeshift executive in a "Ständestaat"' (*op. cit.*, pp. 439–51), and 'Management of Estates in the 17th century: John de Witt, the States of Holland, and the States-General', *Representative Institutions in Theory and Practice . . . Papers presented . . . to Caroline Robbins* (1970), pp. 131–44. Also useful are P. Geyl, *History of the Low Countries* (1964), S. B. Baxter, *William III* (1966), and R. R. Palmer, *The Age of the Democratic Revolution* (1959), Chapter 11. See also E. H. Kossman's essay 'The Dutch Republic (in the 17th century)' in the *New Cambridge Modern History of Europe*, Vol. 5, Chapter 12. G. J. Renier, *The Dutch Nation* (1944), pp. 20 ff., has a penetrating analysis of the working of the States-General.

POLAND, HUNGARY, AND BOHEMIA

The estates in these countries have attracted much attention from patriotic writers, for the memory of these Diets has been an inspiration during ages of foreign oppression. There is however not a great deal available in the languages of western Europe. *The Cambridge History of Poland to 1696* (1950) has a section, pp. 416–40, on 'Constitutional Conditions in the Fifteenth and Sixteenth Centuries', by Professor J. Siemienski. More useful is the essay by Juliusz Bardach entitled 'Gouvernants et Gouvernés en Pologne au Moyen Age et aux temps modernes' in *Recueils Société Jean Bodin*, Vol. 25 (1965), pp. 255–85, a volume which also contains a valuable study of 'The Hungarian feudal diet (13th–18th centuries)' by György Bónis, pp. 287–307. There are stimulating discussions of the Polish Diet in J. Bardach, 'Etat polonais du haut moyen âge', *Acta Poloniae Historica*, V (1962); G. Labuda, 'L'intégration et la désintégration dans l'histoire du premier état polonais', *Studi in onore di A. Fanfani*, Vol. I (1962); Z. Wojciechowski, 'La condition des nobles et le problème de la féodalité en Pologne au moyen âge', *Revue Historique de Droit Français et Etranger*, 4th series, Vol. 15 (1956); J. Dabrowski, 'Corona Regni Poloniae im XIV Jahrhundert', *Corona Regni – Studien über die Krone als Symbol des Staates im späteren Mittelalter* (1961). Three valuable essays on the Hungarian Diet are to be found in the volume presented to the Stockholm Congress of Historians in 1960, *Etudes historiques publiées par la Commission Nationale des Historiens Hongrois*, Vol. 1. The essays are: E. Lederer, 'La structure de la société hongroise au début du Moyen Age'; E. Mályusz, 'Die Zentralisationsbestrebungen König Sigismunds in Ungarn'; L. Elekes, 'Essai de centralisation de l'Etat hongrois dans la seconde moitié du XV siècle'. In *L'Organisation corporative du Moyen Age à la fin de l'Ancien Régime*, Vol. III (1939) F. Eckhart discussed 'La diète corporative hongroise' and E. Mályusz, 'Die Entstehung der Stände im mittelalterlichen Ungarn', pp. 13–30, 211–24, and in *International Commission Studies*, Vols. 18 and 24 (1958 and 1961), pp. 77–122, 347–58, J. Holub has written on 'La représentation politique en Hongrie au Moyen Age' and 'La formation des deux Chambres de l'Assemblée nationale hongroise'.

For Bohemia consult three essays by V. Vanecek: 'Trois catégories d'assemblées d'états dans la couronne de Bohême au XVIᵉ siècle', in *Album Helen Cam*, Vo. 1 (1960), pp. 203–18; 'Les assemblées d'états en Bohême à l'époque de la révolte d'états' in *Recueils Société Jean Bodin*, Vol. 25 (1965), pp. 239–54; 'La situation des états en Bohême entre 1620–1648' in *Mélanges Antonio Marongiu* (1966), pp. 247–58.

An interesting essay by K. Górski, 'Les débuts de la représentation de la Communitas Nobilium dans les assemblées d'états de l'est européen', in *Ancien Pays et Assemblées d'Etats*, 47 (1968), pp. 37–54, compares especially developments in East Prussia, Poland, and Hungary in the fifteenth century.

SCANDINAVIA

For the general background L. Musset's *Les Peuples Scandinaves au Moyen Age* (1951) is helpful. Stewart Oakley's *The Story of Sweden* (1966) and *The Story of Denmark* (1972) provide a good up-to-date survey of the history of these two countries, with good bibliographies. These books can usefully be supplemented by L. Krabbe's *Histoire de Danemark* (1950) and C. Hallendorff and A. Schuck, *History of Sweden* (1929). R. Fusilier provides a brief comparative study of the development of the Scandinavian parliaments in *Les monarchies parlementaires* (1960). There are two short essays by Erik Lönnroth: 'Representative Assemblies of Medieval Sweden', in *International Commission Studies*, Vol. 18 (1958), pp. 123–32, and 'Government in Medieval Scandinavia' in *Recueils Société Jean Bodin*, Vol. 24 (1966), pp. 453–60.

For the later period there is a very useful article by N. Kisliakoff Dumont, 'La Royauté et les Etats en Suède aux XVIIe et XVIIIe siècles (1639–1772)', in *Etudes sur l'Histoire des Assemblées d'états* (Aix-en-Provence, 1964), ed. Fr. Dumont, pp. 37–46. An interesting discussion of the Age of Liberty, analytical rather than chronological, is provided by Sven Ulric Palme, 'The Bureaucratic Type of Parliament: The Swedish Estates during the Age of Liberty, 1719–1772', in *Liber Memorialis Georges de Lagarde* (1968), pp. 239–57.

SCOTLAND

The Acts of the Parliament of Scotland were published in 12 volumes by the Record Commissioners (1814–75) and edited by T. Thomson and C. Innes. The *Records of the Convention of the Royal Burghs of Scotland* were edited by J. D. Marwick in 6 volumes (1870 to 1890). R. S. Rait wrote an authoritative book, *The Parliaments of Scotland*, in 1924, and T. Pagan published an interesting account, *The Convention of Royal Burghs*, in 1926. J. D. Mackie and G. S. Pryde connected the two in *The Estates of the Burgesses in the Scots parliament and its relation to the Convention of Royal Burghs* (1923). Useful articles on the Scottish parliament will be found in many issues of the *Scottish Historical Review*.

SWITZERLAND

There is a good introduction to the subject by F. Gilliard, 'Gouvernés et Gouvernants dans la confédération helvétique, des origines à la fin de l'ancien régime' in *Recueils Société Jean Bodin*, Vol. 25 (1965), pp. 139–61. Further information will be found in A. Heusler, *Schweizerische Verfassungsgeschichte* (1920), of which the first part was translated by G. Abravanel and J. G. Favey in 1924 as *Histoire de des constitutions suisses*. For the general background, see C. Gilliard, *Histoire de la Suisse* (3rd ed., 1961), translated by D.L.B. Harley as *A History of Switzerland* (1955) and G.R. Potter, H.S. Offler, and E. Bonjour, *A Short History of Switzerland* (1952). For a fascinating analysis of the effect of the teachings of Rousseau and Voltaire on the class and constitutional struggles in Geneva in the 1760s, see R.R. Palmer, *The Age of the Democratic Revolution* (1959), pp. 119–39.

ITALY

There is an excellent introduction by A. Marongiu, first published in 1949 as *L'istituto parlamentare in Italia*, for the centenary of the Italian parliament. To explain the growth of the Italian parliament Professor Marongiu examined the rise and development of parliamentary institutions also in Spain, England, France, and Germany. The book was translated into English in 1968 by S.J. Woolf under the title *Medieval Parliaments: a Comparative Study*, but over a third of the book is concerned with Italian parliaments, including an appendix on Italian parliaments of the seventeenth and eighteenth centuries. It has ten pages of bibliography for the Italian parliaments, which the inquirer who wishes to investigate the subject further should consult. For Sicily, where the parliament proved to have more staying power than in any other Italian state, see H.G. Koenigsberger, *The Government of Sicily under Philip II of Spain* (1951), and the same author's *Estates and Revolutions: Essays in Early Modern European History* (1971). The general background of Sicilian history is treated by D.M. Smith, *A History of Medieval Sicily, 800 to 1713* (1968). This is useful for the constitutional history of the state, but its value is limited by the absence of a bibliography, which has been left to the next volume.

ACKNOWLEDGMENTS

Albertina, Vienna, 52; Archivo Corona Aragon, Barcelona, 28; Barcelona Cathedral, 41; Bayerische Staatsbibliothek, Munich, 2; Bern. Histor. Museum, Bern, 75; Biblioteca Nacional, Madrid, 24; Bibliothèque Nationale, Paris, 12, 17, 31, 32, 39, 43, 66; Bibliothèque Royale, Brussels, 1, 68, 69; British Library, 9, 10, 11, 14, 18, 25, 30; Cappella degli Scrovegni, Padua, 8; Corpus Christi College, Cambridge, 22; Drottningholm Castle, Stockholm, 77; Escorial, 27; Foto MAS, 15, 27, 71; Giraudon, 62; Gripsholm Castle, Sweden, 19; Kungl. Biblioteket, Stockholm, 50, 76; Kunsthistorisches Museum, Vienna, 13; Landesarchiv Appenzell, 6; Landesbildstelle Württemberg, Stuttgart, 3; Lauros Giraudon, 42; London Museum, 79; Louvre, Paris, 65; Mansell Collection, 67, 72; Mauritshuis, The Hague, 57; Musée d'Aix, France, 62; Musée des Augustins, Toulouse, 7; Musée Carnavalet, Paris, 60; Musée Dauphinois, Grenoble, 64; Musée de Picardie, Amiens, 63; Museo Historia Ciudad, Barcelona, 15; Museo Municipal, Madrid, 53; Nationalbibliothek, Vienna, 23; National Gallery, London, 34; Nationalmuseum, Stockholm, 37, 49, 51, 77; National Museum, Warsaw, 54, 55; National Portrait Gallery, London, 21, 78; New College, Oxford, 5; Novosti Press Agency, London, 20; Österreichisches Barockmuseum, Vienna, 47; Palais Granvelle, Besançon, 56; Photo Nationalmuseum, Stockholm, 19; Photo Schweizer Landesmuseum, Zürich, 38; Prado, Madrid, 40, 74; Private collection, 61; Rijksmuseum, Amsterdam, 16, 59; Rosenborg Castle, Copenhagen, 48; Royal College of Surgeons of England, London, 4; St Denis, Paris, 29; Staatsbibliothek, Berlin, 73; State Historical Museum, Moscow, 20; William Rockhill Nelson Gallery, Kansas City, 46; Württembergisches Landesmuseum, Stuttgart, 33.